CORN PONE*

*CORN PONE ('KORN-PONE')
half-baked, half-fried staple corn bread patties.

Jimmie McWilliams

D.R. Virtue Press

Copyright © 1992 by J.W. McWilliams
D.R. Virtue Press
ISBN 0-9633194-1-8
Printed in the U.S.A.

All rights reserved. No part of this book may be reproduced or transmitted in any form without the express written permission of the Publisher, except where permitted by law. For information, contact D.R. Virtue Press

---

D.R. Virtue Press
Route 2, Box 342, Cherokee, AL, USA 35616

Table of Contents

Preliminary	1
Dad's Old Hat	3
The Deafening Silence	7
Katie's Gift	11
Monster Cat	15
The "Pantuh" Scare	19
The Brick Haul	23
We Brushed Mama's Hair	27
The Convalescence	29
M. Cheevie III: Deceased	35
His Grandfather's Eyes	39
The Rapture at the Dippin' Vat	43
The Cornfield Mutiny	49
A Dog Tale - Or - A Tale Told by a Wag	55
The End of Summer	59
Readin', 'Ritin' & 'Rithmetic	67
The Great "Lime" Disaster	73
Eddie Was Not A Coward	77
Mamaw's Unfinished Quilts	81
The Clovis Point	87
Maturity?	95

Dad's Old Ledger	99
Ol' Glugly	109
Ol' Blackie and Ol' Blue	113
Ol' Glugly and the Coyote Bitch	119
Memories	125
The Floatin' Gang	131
Orilla's Secret	137
The Treasure Trove	143
Sliced Light Bread	151
G.T.T. (Gone To Texas)	157
Home From the War	163
A Message to Miss Miller	169
The Town's Clown	173
"Tar" Peterson	181
Sam and the Dinner Bell	187
The Ultimate Compliment	193
The Christmas of 1929	199
Rocks In Our Yard or Stone Unhinged	205
The Reunion	211
About the Author - By the Author	215

Preliminary

Cornpone began with a few short items written for a monthly bulletin. A friend, the editor, proofread these items and shielded me from my errors in punctuation, word usage, spelling, sentence structure, etc. I appreciate the help.
Later, my sisters, younger than I, requested stories from our childhood years, years that were beyond their memories' grasp.
Then the local college offered courses in creative writing to senior citizens at a minimum cost. I enrolled. My writing deficiencies were blatantly exposed and my pride deflated. I found it to be true: "Pride doth goeth before a fall."
Now, from my new and more realistic perspective, I continue attempts at writing. For sure, paper, time and ink are expended and cliches are transformed into sentences. A friend jokingly explained it, "The muses spoke and you wrote." Something gets lost in the translation, however, because ink and paper never reflect what is desired.
Older and a little wiser, I offer <u>Cornpone</u> as an unfinished raw effort and put it to rest. At least, I hope it will rest.
The accomplished reader may regard some of the material as overly sentimental, even maudlin. However, reac-

tion from a few acquaintances has been encouraging, with only a few changes suggested. A common bond seems to recognize the emotional threads entwined in the stories.

Remember, it is fiction; because memory is too hazy, too unreliable, too subjective for freehand factual writing. Some stories are based on actual events but all are changed, either purposefully or inadvertently because of poor memory. There is an occasional grain of truth; if you discover it, savor it.

A few friends were "trapped" into early readings that were, in reality, proof-readings. All comments, corrections or suggestions were valuable contributions.

Friends, I thank you.

An added note: Sarah's support continues and is appreciated. A wife's grasp of intention is often better than your own design.

Also, Mary and Cindy have continued the word-processing for several months. This has been over and above expectations. Their acceptance of inconvenience, the illegible and the many changes were met with poise and assurance.

Mr. Nicholas Winn's contribution has been extremely beneficial. He reminded me, again and again, to do better. Thanks again, "Nick".

Thank you, Mary, Cindy, and Nick.

The wastebasket's ravenous, salivating maw crouches there. Reader, please let him go hungry.

Dad's Old Hat

It continues to hang there by the back door on the hat rack. My Mother gave it to me a few years after Dad's death and only a month before she also died. I brought it home and hung it there.

The straw hat is faded and the band area is sweat-stained. There is a hole up front on the crown where his dirt and sweat-stained fingers would grasp it for removal or adjustment. When the hat was new, there was a tag inside with, "size 7½, price $2.00", written on it; it is unreadable now. A few of the red hairs from his head are caught in the straw of the crown.

I can visualize him now: with hoe in hand and a red bandanna hanging from his overall's hip pocket, he is standing in his garden as I drive up in my pick-up. He yells, "The corn is ready for the freezer. I'll have two hundred ears ready at 6:30 tomorrow morning." I stop for a visit and he gives his instructions, "Be here before seven o'clock because I have some wood to haul and stack." He continues, "This is the best corn crop I've ever grown," and his good-natured pervasive grin spreads over his ruddy face beneath the old straw hat's brim. "Are you going to town?" he asks. "I need some turnip green seeds for a fall 'salate' crop."

His recreation was always some productive project. His goal, his incentive was always the creation of something useful. He never sat with the "whittlin' and spittin'" club, and his idle talk was usually humorous. Nor did he fit any stereotype of an elderly farmer. His only reason for wasteful rest was recuperation in preparation for tomorrow's project.

His brother, Uncle Andy, and he bought and operated the first farm tractor in Colbert County. He with a team of mules, was the first to start leveling a railroad right-of-way to the Wilson Dam building area. There is a picture of him with a motorcycle gang in 1911. Lieutenant (later General) Doolittle picked him as his flight crew chief during World War I because of his expertise in gasoline engines. The first lime spread on an alfalfa patch in his community was on land owned by his family. He helped build churches, served on the boards of farm agencies, pioneered new farming practices, and always tried to be optimistic, even during the depression of the thirties.

At age ninety, his body betrayed him. One hot day, with hoe in hand and the old straw hat on his head, he had a stroke out in his garden. He rode to the hospital under protest.

The outer visible man never recovered. He was lost to us forever; but the inner stronger man lived on for five more years.

There were a few times when he fought back for brief periods of almost complete remembrance. Occasionally, eye contact affirmed his love for us, but these periods were brief and his inner strength was gradually smothered by the dark dismal confusion of the stroke. He gradually faded from us over a long five-year period. It was not his nature to give up. He was a survivor. He never surrendered.

We buried him on a cold, snowy day in March. It was just before spring and garden planting time.

The old straw hat with the red hair caught in the crown still remains on the hat rack by the back door - it just hangs in there.

The Deafening Silence

Every sound shall end in silence, but the silence never dies ...
                                    Hegerman 1848 - 1905

There was a silence deep as death, and the boldest held his breath for a while ...
                                    Campbell 1777 - 1844

A SCALED-DOWN REPLICA of the Vietnam War Memorial is being revealed to many communities throughout America. It was recently displayed just off Highway 72 in Tuscumbia, Alabama.

Most people drove past with only a casual glance; it was part of the American past. We had seen it many times through the eyes of the news media. Why see it again?

However, one hot sunny afternoon, on the spur of the moment, I stopped to visit "The Wall."

There was no crowd. Registration was unhindered and shortly I found myself standing before The Wall, completely unprepared for what I was about to experience.

All those names!

Most had been young, just kids, and their names ran for many yards before the viewer. The numb, unspoken reproach of all those unlived lives could not be ignored. The plight of us the living became vulnerable, exposed - tenuous.

All those hundreds of names!

Wilted flowers lay strewn along the base of The Wall. A few dusty pictures leaned against it. A worn teddy bear and a frayed security blanket had been returned to their rightful owners. Two bronzed baby shoes reflected the bright sunlight. An envelope had come unstuck and revealed the words, "— still love you."

All those thousands of names!

Perhaps twenty people stood before The Wall. Some were alone, others were in groups. All stood in absolute silence. The only sound came from the nearby traffic. The heat from the sun on the dark wall shimmered as though The Wall were alive. It was!

All the thousands of lives touched by those names!

A grandfatherly man and a younger middle-aged man stood side-by-side convulsed in grief and memory. A family group stood in a semi-circle. An elderly lady attempted to focus a camera through a veil of tears. Four veterans of that war, dressed in camouflage fatigues, stood arm-in-arm near the midpoint.

The shimmering from the wall increased!

A lady, near the far end, stood with her head inclined as though listening to The Wall; a nurse's insignia was attached to her lapel. She shed no comforting tears as she stood motionless in the silence - listening.

And then I heard:

There was the whoosh-whoosh-whoosh of helicopters, the brrrr-brrrr-brrrrr of machine and gatling guns, the pop-pop-pop of rifle fire, the concussion of grenades, the earth-shattering explosion of bombs, the shouts, the whine of motors, the screams of pain, the zing-zing of ricocheting shrapnel, the gurgle of chest wounds, the moans of the dying, and the overall roar of war. There was also the smell of fear, of blood, of excrement, of gun powder, of engine exhaust, of rotting flesh, of sweat, of putrid vegetation, of foul water and of fear. Closed eyes could see the scene clearly. There were the mangled bodies - friend and foe together - entangled in grotesque display and over it all the miasma of death rose like a dank and dismal fog.

The silence was unbearable!

I fled in measured pace back to the entrance. As I escaped, I glanced back. The lady with the nurse's insignia still stood - listening in the deafening silence.

Katie's Gift

S̲HE IS EIGHT-YEARS-YOUNG, going on eighteen, and we are "baby-sitting" again. Katie had a fever from a virus and had to stay home from school. Both parents are working and a happy grandfather has a pleasant chore for the day - once again.

In our headlong rush through time, occasionally an event comes 'round again and a sense of deja vu causes a day to seem the same as a day of long ago; a day that was bliss, a day long remembered and the day Katie gave me the stick that is taped to my picture down the hallway.

- - -

That day, six years ago, found Katie and me together again. She was two-years-young and I was "thirty-nine-and- holding." It was before my retirement and there were chores away from the farm. We rode in the pick-up all morning in animated conversation, play, and indulgence. At mid-morning, her bright brown eyes fluttered, snapped shut and she collapsed into a sleeping blonde heap on the seat. I untangled her limbs and hair as she contentedly continued a kittenish snoring. When we rolled to a stop in the carport, she bounced up instantly and announced, "I'm hungry and I need to go to the bathroom, right now."

After a short pit stop, we returned to the pick-up with a box of eating goodies and drove to the cow pasture. There were some buckeyes in the ash tray. Katie examined them and decided that we should gather some more.

It was a beautiful October day and the trees were nearby. We found an empty box and within minutes we were picking buckeyes.

As we were gathering, I became aware of a third party to our expedition because Katie was talking animatedly to someone named Billy. She instructed Billy to put them in the basket and then continued, "You missed those two under your foot, Billy." I assumed that Billy was a fantasy and moved toward Katie to eavesdrop. Then I saw Billy: He was a short stick in Katie's left hand, about six inches long with a knot for a head and two twig-like arms. His puppet-like gyrations in her hand were a wonder. Billy gathered buckeyes as well as Katie.

We soon filled our boxes and returned to the kitchen for another snack. Billy ate half a peanut butter cracker and three drops of milk. Then it was nap time again. Both Billy and Katie were tucked in bed and slept until Katie's mother came for her.

She was a drowsy sleepy-head when she awoke and forgot Billy, until she was being led out the door. Then she remembered her little friend and ran back for him. As she cradled Billy in her arms, she realized that he was "our" secret friend. She turned and gently gave him to me with the admonition, "You keep Billy so you will have a little friend to go with you tomorrow."

- - -

But today when we walked down the hallway Katie inquired, "Why is that stick taped to your picture, Buddy Pal?" I attempted an explanation and found that she had no memory of Billy. In fact, in her eight-year-old sophistica-

tion, she probably thought my story a little strange.
But Billy and I remember - and understand.

Monster Cat

EVERY FARM in the 1920s - '30s had a passel (or is it a pride?) of cats. This was especially true before and during the depression era.

During those years, cats made their own way in the world and often came begging at milking time or meal time for an occasional handout. But, mostly they lived by foraging for mice, birds, lizards, and other small animals. In today's world they would have been labeled as "feral" animals.

These were the circumstances that brought about a reign of terror by a tomcat that became known as "Monster."

Hogs had been slaughtered in early December that year and the smell of blood and meat had attracted the local passel of cats, including Monster, who made his new home in the hay mow of the mule barn and then lived "high on the hog" during the slaughter period. He was as large as a small bobcat and because of his size soon intimidated the local tomcats into groveling retreat. His grey color blended into the landscape so he was seldom seen. He became a true phantom of the farm. We farm folk welcomed his presence because we expected litters of super kittens.

The hog-killing had progressed smoothly during the

cold crisp days. Sausage, lard, hog-head cheese, cracklings, chitterlings, hams, bacon, shoulders, pork-chops, and the other products of an efficient slaughter were all ready for good eating. The hams, shoulders, and side meat bacon were removed from the salt cure and were hung high, with baling wire, from the smokehouse rafters.

It was then that Monster became addicted to smokehouse meat. At first, the gnawed meat was blamed on rats but no rat droppings or tracks were present. The squirrels' agility made them a prime suspect, but no squirrels were seen. Someone mentioned coons as a likely suspect but again; there were no coon tracks. Then Monster's pilfering was confirmed when he was seen leaving the smokehouse one morning at dawn.

Dad attempted to stop all the cracks and holes in the smokehouse walls, doors, and ceilings, but Monster continued to find new ways to feast on smokehouse meat.

Finally, Dad installed an electric light, set his alarm clock for 1:00 a.m. and placed a stout hickory club by the smokehouse door.

Dad caught Monster the next morning red-handed (or red pawed?). When the light went on Monster sat atop a ham gnawing away. Dad swung at him while he was on the ham. It was a glancing blow that had little effect, and Monster leaped to the floor but in his confusion, he forgot his exit route.

A battle raged. Monster ran from wall to wall with Dad in pursuit. Monster ran up the wall, leaped to the hanging meat and ran from ham to ham, from shoulder to ham, from shoulder to shoulder, to side meat, to the wall again, and then repeated the route with Dad following each move with a constant rain of blows. Dad shouted; Monster snarled, meowed, growled, and spat; the club smashed and beat. The noise reverberated under the tin roof like the sound of a drunken riot. Both combatants soon ran out of adrenaline and lapsed into life and death desperation. Monster changed his tactics into a gorilla routine. He pounced from a ham onto Dad's shoulder, ran up Dad's leg and leaped to the wall, then back onto Dad's head. Then he circled and tried to climb Dad's back. Dad lost his hat and realized the exposure of his bald head. The situation had changed and needed rethinking. Dad's shotgun came to mind, and he attempted to slip out the door quickly and leave Monster inside, but Monster was no dummy; he leaped to Dad's back and rode him to freedom.

Monster went "cold turkey" to smokehouse meat; we never saw him again. However, during the following four years, no tomcat was seen on our farm. Yet we regularly had litters of super kittens from our female cats.

The "Pantuh" Scare

The "Whittlin' and Spittin' Club" sat around the stove in the back of Boss Keeton's store and came to the conclusion that it was a "pantuh." One old timer, Harv Rutledge, recalled, "My papa said he shot a pantuh that was killin' our calves back in 1880." He continued, "They had to wipe 'em cats out cause they was about to take over."

In 1927 there were no panthers left in the Southeastern United States except for a few in the Smokies and the Everglades. The deer, bear, and turkey were also gone from the hills of North Alabama. It was all an open range for cattle, who could roam at will; cattlemen could not permit the competition of too much wildlife.

Anyway, rumor fed on rumor and soon a "pantuh" scare was upon us. It all began when Orville Jones's fattening pig vanished. Then Tom Clam's heifer had claw marks on her back. The rumor became certainty when Jake Watkins heard a "pantuh" scream down on Mulberry Creek. He said it sounded, "Just like my wife when she spilled that hot lard on her foot last winter."

Within a week the rumor had spread from the Whittlin' and Spittin' " Club to the far ends of the county. Its rapidity of communication would put our modern telephone system to shame.

The rumor became a certified certainty when an "expert" reported that animals from the Smokies did indeed roam for hundreds of miles and often became established in new ranges.

And then, one morning at 2:00 a.m., our dogs, Collie, Fritz, and Yap, began their "extreme terror" alarm bark. (Now rural people and dogs have an understanding about barking. Most dogs have a repertoire that ranges from ordinary to extreme terror bark. The ordinary is an answer to the dog on the next farm, or an announcement that the moon has risen, or that a rabbit squeaked or even that he had a dream. Then there is the "need help" bark when a 'possum is in the chicken house or when a strange person is arriving. And then there is the terror alarm, the bark that is the equivalent of human screams for help.)

The dog's terror alarm woke everyone. Dad leaped out of bed, grabbed his old thirty-eight Smith & Wesson revolver from the top drawer of the chiffonier, and ran in his B.V.D.'s out to the side porch to rescue the dogs. The light from the porch frightened the attacker away. Dad opened the screen door and had no target to shoot. He sicked the dogs into the dark yard, where they caught up to their antagonist. The battle was rejoined: The howling, snarling, snapping, biting pack retreated back to the porch. When they reached the circle of light, our dogs fled in headlong retreat to the security of Dad's presence. He waited until the dogs were behind him and set himself for the slaughter. The pursuing animal hesitated when it came into the circle of light and Dad aimed and pulled the trigger. I remember it well: the old gun went, "click - click - clickeliekelick". Dad yelled, howled, and hollered as he slammed the screen door open, fell into the hallway and kicked the solid oak door shut. Then he fled to the bathroom and soon we heard him flush the commode.

When he came out, he dressed, even though it was not yet 4:00 a.m. and milking time. He found that the old gun had been unloaded for safe storage and was also rusty. A can of machine oil and reloading soon had it ready for the "pantuh" if it should return.

But Dad confessed that he did not know what had attacked the dogs. "It was a black shape", is all he knew for certain.

Our dogs had a few scratches, but no wounds of consequence; however, one observant woodsman, upon seeing the scratches, thought they were made by another dog. "Perhaps a lost coon hound lookin' for something to eat."

The "pantuh" rumor ran rampant for a few days after Dad's encounter and then gradually died from lack of more evidence.

Two weeks later the "Whittlin' and Spittin' " Club spat on the sizzling stove just after Josh pushed a hickory chunk into it.

Clem allowed as how, "That Jergenson gal has moved back into their ol' home place."

And Orville remembered, "Yeah, las' night I seen her drive by in that ol' Model T Ford of her'n well past midnight."

Jake added, "I'll bet she's still seein' that judge's boy over at the county seat. Why, I ain't never seen such — ."

The Brick Haul

WHEN WE MOVED to the old Goodloe home and farm in 1926, we found that most of the buildings were in chronic disrepair. The old brick smokehouse had an end wall completely missing because of pilfering for chimney repair to other buildings.

Dad decided to rebuild it, if possible, with matching brick. After inquiry, he found an abandoned chimney that fit the need in Sheffield. He bought it, and soon had the bricks cleaned, stacked, and ready for hauling.

The depression of post World War I was still remembered, so he decided to save hauling costs by moving a few brick each day when he returned from his milk delivery.

Within a week he had moved seven hundred brick with no problems - and no cost. Saturday arrived and there were five hundred bricks remaining. Now, Saturday is a special day for rural folk. It makes us optimistic - and reckless. So Dad decided to move the last bricks in one big load.

However, his old 1923 Dodge truck, nicknamed "Ol' Streak" was rated as a one-half ton vehicle. It had wooden spoked wheels that were twenty-five inches in diameter so the truck would ride above the ruts, rocks, and other obstacles of the gravel roads of those days. There were band type brakes, on only the rear wheels, that were prone to overheating and failure. In those times all loaded trucks eased downhill in low gear to avoid runaway. The cab resembled a horse-drawn buggy with canvas closures for rain and winter driving. Tires often blew and punctures were an almost daily occurrence. Tires were also expensive by the standards of those times. We should add that the wooden spokes groaned and squeaked under an overload.

But it was Saturday and Ol' Streak soon groaned under five hundred bricks, the empty milk cans and Dad's one hundred ninety pounds.

The journey home began with squeaky wheels, bulging tires and a laboring motor. They ground up Lily Pond hill, crept down Baker Lane, coasted through Cane Creek bottom, eased down and out of Gatesville Creek Ford, and finally stopped an hour later at Boss Keeton's general store for five gallons of regular gas. Boss pumped up five and as it drained into Ol' Streak, he noted, "Bill, you've really got a load." He continued, "You know bricks weigh 'bout ten pounds. How many you haulin'?"

"Five hundred," was the reply.

Boss grinned. "Why, that's pushin' three tons - five hundred bricks, and the cans, and you, and five gallons of gas! Better unload half those bricks and come back for them later."

But it was Saturday, so Dad paid Boss five dimes for the gas and crept on home in fear and dread. The squeaking wheels, laboring motor, popping gravel, and other sounds were amplified by Boss' revelation and Dad's anticipation of disaster.

Meanwhile at home, I had eaten dinner (mid-day meal) and picked up a handful of matches to shoot some firecrackers I had found in the pocket of my old winter coat. Then I heard Dad and Ol' Streak creeping up the hill.

Dad drove past the house slowly and carefully and then maneuvered so as to back into position to unload by the brick pile. Dad's head protruded from the cab, in his attempt to see exactly where he was backing as he carefully negotiated each foot of the way.

I became bored with all that slow careful driving and turned my attention to the firecrackers. An old five gallon can sat next to the brick pile so I lighted a fuse and dropped a "cracker" into the can. Now, how was I to know that it was an old gas can? The resulting explosion was a major event. "KKKKKAAAAABBBLLLL-OOOOMMMM", it went.

Dad cut the ignition on Ol' Streak, leaped to the ground, jerked off his hat, stomped it, stomped it again and circled the truck fast. Then he circled it slowly again; and, in doubt, he circled it once more and kicked each tire. He raised the hood flaps from both sides to check the motor. He crawled under Ol' Streak and shook the hot muffler. He retrieved his hat, shook out the wrinkles, scratched his head, and replaced the hat.

As he readjusted it, he noticed me sitting on the brick pile. "Did you hear that?", he inquired.

"What?", I answered innocently.

"That loud KKKAAAABBBLLLOOOMMM", he mimicked.

"That was just a firecracker I shot", I quavered in a small depreciating voice.

"You what? Shot a firecracker? Why? Why just now?", he demanded.

"Cause I had it", was my reasoning.

The humor of the situation overcame anger and he grinned. "Don't ever do that again, especially when I'm backing a loaded truck", he admonished.

"How 'bout if it's half loaded", was my smart-ass reply.

It was a reply that I regretted more and more as I unloaded the truck - brick by ten-pound brick.

We Brushed Mama's Hair

SHE CALLED THE BOY and his two sisters; they responded immediately and found her sitting before a mirror brushing her hair. She hugged the three together and then asked them to take turns brushing her hair. The boy was six; his sisters were four and two. A baby brother lay in a nearby crib.

Her hair was red-brown, shoulder length and cool to the touch as they brushed it. When each child brushed, she held the other two to her side in a firm embrace.

The ritual was interrupted when their Grandmother arrived to take them for a weekend visit. She collected a paper poke of clothing for each child and then the two women conferred for several minutes. The Grandmother came away pale, drawn and teary-eyed. Then the mother again summoned the boy and his sisters to her chair and hugged each in turn and clung persistently to their hands as they were led away. They saw her waving behind the window curtains as they were driven off.

She had attempted to explain to the boy the reason for a return to the hospital after only a few days at home. He remembered the words "appendicitis", "peritonitis", and "might be gone a long time"; but it was all meaningless to a six-year-old's mind.

The Grandmother left the boy at his aunt's because she had boys his age and let the sisters visit other kinfolk's homes. They never noticed the quiet discussions among the grown-ups nor did they question the sad faces and tear-reddened eyes of those days.

Until one morning Aunt Mary was sobbing uncontrollably as she added wood to the fireplace fire. When asked what was wrong, she answered in agony, "Your Mama died last night." The boy had no conception of death or else refused to accept the finality it implied. His mind erased most of that day from memory and little is remembered of that day or night.

The next day the boy and his sisters saw her lying in a box. She seemed serene and at peace. Later the boy remembers standing behind the grown-ups as they lowered the box into the red clay soil of the local cemetery. He looked back as they were driven away and saw them shoveling the red clay back in place.

It was then that the boy knew that "she might be gone a long time."

The boy cannot recall much of those days. Just a few scenes return to memory on occasion. A long procession of all black cars, the events at the cemetery, the return home and a long visit at Grandma's house.

The boy would confirm that we all waved "Good-bye" when we left - after we brushed Mama's hair.

More than half a century later she returned in the boy's dreams, took his hand, and she and the boy walked down a quiet country lane. No words were spoken - it was just a walk together. He awoke with acceptance.

The Convalescence

THE NURSE'S AIDE wheeled him to the side of the phone booth, gave him the phone, and asked for the number again. The quarters fed into the slot and he heard the usual, "Ding, Ding, Ding," then the "Burr, Burr, Burr," of the answering phone. His hands were sweaty and his heart changed to a "Thud, Thud, Thud" beat. Except for his mother and the nurses, he had not spoken to a woman for months.

And then a pleasant young womanly voice came on. "Hello," it said.

Bob forgot his religiously prepared speech and stammered, "H..H..Hello." Then he continued, "I'm Bob Raven. I was Joseph Smith's friend and....." He caught his breath and hesitatingly inquired, "Are you Mary Smith? Wife of Joseph Smith?"

There was a long silence and then, "Yes, I am, and you are Joe's friend from the Marines and Vietnam? I remember you from his letters." There was a hesitation and then she continued, "before he was killed. Where are you now?"

He regained his composure and answered in his flat Oklahoma drawl, "I'm in the Veterans' Hospital in Los Angeles. Joseph - Joe - asked me to phone you if I could. It's been a long time, but the doctor said I should wait until I was stronger."

"What did Joe? How? Why did he...?" she attempted to ask.

He broke in, "I can have visitors this week-end, I'm told, and I'm no good at phone conversation. Would you... could you drive up from San Diego?"

"Yes, of course I'll be there." was her prompt reply.

"Joe asked me to..." his voice broke, but he struggled on. "He asked me to visit you, but I can't until they fit me with a new leg. It'll take a month or more, I'm told. The hospital is on Wilshire Boulevard, at 11302." He repeated the address and then explained that gangrene had destroyed his leg and prevented him from phoning, after his return to the States.

"But you did phone," she countered, "and I'll see you this week-end. Would Saturday afternoon about one o'clock be OK?"

"Saturday at one will be fine. By the way, I'm in Ward B."

"Then I'll see you there. Good-bye."

Bob spent the next few days in anticipation tempered with apprehension. A look in the mirror confirmed his suspicions: He had lost so much. His eyes were sunken orbs peering from a wrinkled, cadaverous-looking face. His one hundred ten pounds, down from his normal two hundred six, made his body appear as a brown parchment-covered skeleton.

The visiting barber trimmed his hair and a shave uncovered more wrinkles. The mustache was left because he imagined that it made him appear older and more mature than his twenty-one years. It also disguised the lines of suffering around his mouth. He would keep the mustache the rest of his life.

His mother, an Indian who was a school nurse and school bus driver from Ardmore, Oklahoma, had visited him within days of his hospitalization in Los Angeles. The fever from the gangrene was ravaging his body and mind at the time. She calmed him and possibly saved his life by restoring his will to live. The delirium had erased most of the memory of her visit except for a few phrases: "Bob, you and I have been together since before you were born. When I divorced Lacey, you were all I had left. I'll always be thinking of you. By the way, when Lavenia divorced you, she turned around and married that sheriff's son over in Barlow County. They had a baby four months later. Bob, there's no turning back. Remember the old Indian saying, 'Every journey starts from here.' I love you, Bob." Her words and presence had helped restore his sense of reality and desire to live.

The terror of Vietnam would return on occasion. He could recall the blast, the concussion, but nothing more. When consciousness had returned, he had been in a muddy ditch half-covered in green scummy water. Joe had tugged urgently at his arm and mumbled, "Bob, I won't make it outta here. If you get out, tell Mary I'm sorry and someday remember me to my little son, Jimmie."

His rescue must have been a day later because he remembered the dark, the cold and groping for Joe in the slimy darkness. He grasped an arm, then the shoulder and head and knew in his confusion the awful fact..... Joe was dead.

He had blinked his eyes open one morning in Ward B. His first words were, "Where's Joe?" A counselor had come to his side and explained that he had been unconscious from shock and sedation for a long time; that he was in a hospital in Los Angeles and was recovering from his injuries. His main injury was the right leg that had been amputated.

The counselor promised to inquire about Joseph Smith and later had returned and reported that the rescue team had brought out only the living. When they returned they discovered that the Cong had hidden the dead. Joe's body was never recovered.

- - -

The medical nurse wheeled her cart into the ward and sedated several amputees before Bob remembered that it was Saturday - Mary Smith's day. When the nurse came to his bed, he held up his hand. "Wait a minute," he implored. "Could we talk before my shot?"

"Of course we can," she replied.

"I'm to have a visitor at one o'clock and I need to be wide awake. It's important. Why not later, after my visitor has gone?"

She hesitated. "Let's check your vital signs first." Then she inquired, "Will you buzz me if the pain is too much?"

"Yes."

"Then I'll wait until two o'clock, no later."

- - -

Mary Smith came into the ward at exactly one o'clock. Benji Bowden, the ward's macho man alerted them by a low cheerful whistle.

"I'm looking for Bob Raven," she had boldly announced.

"I'm Bob. I'm Bob. I'm Bob," were several assertions.

"But I'm the real Bob," he loudly insisted from his bed at one end of the ward.

She beamed from all the male attention and turned to him, "The really real Bob?" she questioned.

"Yes."

His gaunt face was instantly mirrored sympathetically in her concerned smile and she questioned, "Do you feel up to a ride down to the visitors' center? The doctor has given his OK and I have a wheelchair ready. How 'bout it?"

"I'd go anywhere with you," was his gallant answer, and minutes later they were talking in a quiet corner of the visitors' center.

Bob recounted Joe's short life in Vietnam and agonized through the day and night of his death and explained that he knew Joe's body was never recovered. They sat in mutual grief and silence for a time, then Bob explained the obligation he felt to some day tell Joe's son about his father's last words. "If I do that, I'll have to keep in touch," he observed.

Mary instantly answered, "Bob, you were Joe's dear friend; now you are a dear friend to me."

The throbbing ghost pain in his leg was increasing and he asked to be taken back to the ward. Mary moved the chair a few steps, then stopped, bent her face to his, kissed him full on the lips and, without more conversation, returned him to the ward. She bade a brief good-bye and fled to the sanctuary in the visitors' center.

Bob lay unmoving in his bed for a long time until the phantom pain in his missing foot brought him back to earth a half hour later.

"Bob, will you marry me?" she tentatively but boldly asked six months later. Bob had known that Mary should arrive for a visit and in anticipation had been permitted to practice his walking in the parking lot. She saw him first, and drove close behind him, stepped out of the car; and when he turned, she looked him in the eye and asked.

His reply was also direct. "Yes," he answered, "How 'bout right now?" They were married in the visitors' center three days later.

Eight years later little Jimmie, Joe's son, was a towheaded, playful and happy fourth-grader in a San Diego suburb. He had two raven-haired little sisters, ages four and six. The handsome family was a hit at all the Little League games and at the Kindergarten events.

When the Vietnam War Memorial was complete, Bob reminded Mary, "It's time to keep my promise to Joseph. The station wagon runs good so why don't we take a month's vacation? We can visit Mama in Ardmore and take her with us to Washington. She would love to see the kids again and we will take Jimmie to "The Wall" to see Joseph and learn about him." He seriously continued, "His spirit will be there, you know."

Mary, Bob, and Jimmie came to The Wall, early on a Monday morning. Bob had worn his old camouflage fatigues from the Vietnam era. Mary was reluctant. "I'm afraid to open those awful memories," she explained. "But I'll do it for Jimmie's sake."

The three became quiet and subdued as they approached the black marble. It loomed large as life - and death - before them.

There were only a few visitors at The Wall and the attendants directed them to Joseph Smith with no waiting.

Jimmie saw Joseph first. "There he is! There he is! I see him!" he exclaimed. Without speaking, Bob lifted him high enough to place his hand over Joseph Smith and kiss him. Bob, in turn, still holding Jimmie, took Mary's hand in his and placed them over Jimmie's on the black marble.

The four of them clung together for a time in regret and memory, isolated in common grief, sorrow, and family. The comfort of tears came and then they sat silently before Joseph Smith. Later they talked about Joe and Vietnam, and Jimmie knew more about his father's life and death. The four of them became meshed in the common bond of memory.

Later, the three visitors walked away, arm in arm. Bob glanced back and signaled "A-OK" with his free hand.

M. Cheevie III: Deceased

HE WAS TALL, HANDSOME, RICH, AND bored with all of life at age thirty-five. Living had become a burden to his sophisticated taste and he scorned the "ordinary" with vigor. People, especially, often fell victim to his biting sarcasm and disdain. All his appetites were satiated by abundance and in his boredom he roamed about searching for "something of interest."

One morning he awoke with an extreme hangover, as a result of his search, and found life unbearable. While caught up in nausea and distemper, he looked upward and pled, "God, if you will take me out of this vale of tears, I'll gladly die," and then he hastily added, "But only if you place me in an afterlife of my own choosing."

God, knowing M. Cheevie III, instantly replied, "Agreed. You may die today and I'll instruct St. Peter to place you in the kind of afterlife you prefer."

All was done, as agreed, and shortly Cheevie stood before St. Peter's desk. Without any preliminary introduction, Cheevie began a tirade. "I want to dwell in a place that has no vexing sensory stimulation," he began. (It was a phrase he had picked up at one of the many colleges he had attended.) "Make it a quiet nothing. Use the earth as an example and make it as different as possible. I want to live an afterlife of the mind; I want to experience complete introspection. Let me be a guru of total withdrawal," he concluded.

St. Peter finally had a chance to speak and exclaimed, "We can provide you with exactly what you ask. However, before you sign in, let me describe what you are asking of us."

Cheevie interrupted again, "As unlike earth as possible."

St. Peter continued, "It will be a place of complete peace. There will be no vexing weather. There will be no other life forms to bother you. You will be the only living being in this place of perpetual peace - no animals, no birds, no fish, no germs. It will be just you." St. Peter continued, "We will name it <u>Cheevie's Domain</u> and it will be endless in all directions, infinite. The temperature, humidity, light, and other aspects will be as you choose initially; but choose well because it will remain so for all time. The light will be an all pervasive glow. It will be in no way like the sun, moon, stars, or even an aurora. Of course, no sound will disturb you. If you make your own sounds, we will furnish ear plugs to muffle them." St. Peter grinned and added, "Nose plugs also." He thoughtfully continued, "There is the problem of your memory. It may bring back the experience of all the worrisome vexations of earth. If you wish we can erase your memory."

Cheevie was tempted, but on second thought he declined as he reasoned, "If I keep my memory, I can contrast this peaceful place with the misery of earth and enjoy my new domain even more."

"You are so right," St. Peter observed ironically and added, "There is the problem of time. You humans are extremely time-conscious. The domain will be completely time deprived. The passage of time, as you are aware, disturbs the peace. All will be static, still, motionless. No time awareness of any kind to remind you of earth."

Cheevie was almost ecstatic in his anticipation and then

he remembered that he had a body. "How do I get food, drink, clothing and shelter? When? Where? How?" he inquired.

"Those are earthly needs," St. Peter reminded him. "The magic of your new domain is that you always remain as you are. You will need nothing, absolutely nothing. However, though you will not need them, we'll let you wear clothing. Remember, one of your earthly philosophers bared his navel, and its implications gave him much thought. You will need no interfering earthly thoughts so flesh-colored coveralls will be furnished." St. Peter beckoned a lieutenant and concluded, "You are now ready to enter your new domain. We'll watch over you."

M. Cheevie III entered the domain with boundless optimism (a new emotion to him). He let the quiet seep into his being. A soft blue glow permeated it all. The atmosphere and infinitely level plain all blended together and the glow let him see forever in all directions. He felt as though his entire being were immersed in warm water, weightless and at peace. His mind relaxed and gradually became a total blank. There was no awareness of body or mind, or of the domain. <u>Cheevie became nothing at peace with itself.</u>

Until:

A louse egg had escaped the "de-lifeing" process in the preparation chambers. It has been hidden in the wrinkles of his navel. The egg hatched and grew to maturity during Cheevie's distraction with the repose of peace. Later, it crawled onto his nose from his eyebrows and Cheevie captured it between thumb and forefinger. He let it crawl into his palm and gently probed it with the forefinger of his other hand. As it moved about he rotated his wrist to keep it in view as it received his total concentration. He smelled it, listened for sound, caressed it for feel, adjusted it before his eyes for better focus, and even gently tasted the louse with his tongue.

Later the louse crawled up his wrist toward his upper

arm and Cheevie loosened his close-fitted sleeve to admit the louse into his clothing.

A lieutenant from the Personal Hell Division reported to the Devil, "Sir, you know, when St. Peter transferred the Personal Domain Division over to us, it was the right decision. It fits our management policy much better. M. Cheevie III, especially, is better off, even though he has no awareness of the transfer. However, he has ceased wandering about and now spends all his time just lying there. Occasionally, he scratches and adjusts his coveralls. That's all he does."

His Grandfather's Eyes

(This story is essentially true because it reflects much of human experience. It is fiction because it does not reflect accurately a series of specific events.)

Oh dreadful is the shock - Intense the agony, When the ear begins to hear, And the eye begins to see.
Emily Bronte 1818-48

THE BOY stood behind the grown-ups and caught glimpses of the box containing his mother's body, as it was lowered into the red clay soil. He was numb, confused, angry, and had no understanding of the proceedings.

At the conclusion of the ceremonies, his infant brother, sisters aged two and four, and the boy were returned home. The boy was six.

The kinfolk had conferred with the father and it was decided that "the children" should be parceled out to close relatives until the father could regain his composure and provide the care necessary for young ones. The boy's maternal grandmother agreed to keep him because, as she said, "He's old enough for me to care for." A poke of clothing was filled and he accompanied her when she departed for her home. There was no one to wave "Goodbye" as they drove away.

The grandfather was sitting on his front porch when they arrived. He was dressed in his "Sunday-best" black broadcloth suit and wore a sweat-stained and weathered felt hat. His body sat rigidly upright on an old hickory bark-bottomed chair while he grasped a hickory walking stick before him, holding on to it as though it were firmly implanted in the oak planks of the porch floor.

When the boy approached, the old man reached out for him. His walking stick clattered to the floor as he held the boy at arm's length for a moment. He then set him on his knee and looked into the youth's eyes, a long penetrating look. In tenderness he patted the skinny back, hugged the boy briefly, and set him on his feet again. Regaining his hickory cane, he replanted it on the oak floor, and clung to it as though a strong wind were blowing.

The uncomprehending child walked through the house, across the back porch, into the back yard, and then turned and crawled into the dirt under the porch. He remained hidden there until all memory of the day's happenings had been erased. Later, he came out and played drag-the-stick with Ol' Shep, the resident yard-dog. His day ended with darkness, the smell of wood smoke and cornpone, and the oblivion of a warm bed.

Six decades and more have passed since that day. Unprecedented and profound changes have occurred and engaged the boy's attention. Depression, war, mortgages, marriage, family and many other important things required his care and concentration. He remembered no details of the grandfather's death and funeral. It was just one of many funerals he attended over the years.

His grandfather's children and their children were prolific. A recent family reunion would have made him extremely proud and happy. However, if he had appeared and walked among them in modern garb, few would have recognized him. Fewer still would have been aware of his life and times and the part he had played in their well-being.

A short history of his life should be of interest to all his grandchildren: He came from the hills of Appalachia into the Tennessee Valley soon after his marriage. Bride and groom would have been considered as children today. In the late eighteen hundreds they had organized a business founded on timber-cutting and saw-milling. They were diligent in their business and successful in their acquisitions.

Eight children were born to them, but only four survived to the age of thirty. One daughter, a twin, died from whooping cough at age five. An eleven-year-old son succumbed to appendicitis. Another son drowned at age eighteen, when thrown from a horse while herding cattle across a rain-swollen stream. Another daughter, the boy's mother, fell victim to appendicitis when she was twenty-nine, leaving four small children. His surviving children were all successful parents and citizens.

The grandfather's last surviving child died two days ago. She was ninety-two. The boy's Aunt Belle is now interred near her sisters, brothers, and parents.

The boy traveled the long two miles to her grave this morning. He stood in the cemetery and leaned against the grandfather's tombstone just as the clouds parted and the sun began to bathe the area with warmth and light.

And then - the memories came rushing back: The boy crawled from the dirt under the back porch, walked through the house and once again sat upon his grandfather's knee. The old man still wore his Sunday-best black broadcloth suit. The grey, aged felt hat sat squarely on his head, still sweat-stained and weathered. His beard was tobacco-stained and mottled, and his eyes still light brown and tear-brightened. His old hickory stick clattered to the floor and the boy "saw" the grief, the agony, the concern and love in those eyes. Six decades and more were but as a moment to the now comprehending boy. And the boy clung to the tombstone as though a strong wind were blowing.

The Rapture at the Dippin' Vat

Laughter - 'laf-ter n. An interior convulsion producing a distortion of the features and accompanied by a violent expulsion of inarticulate noises.

Ambrose Bierce - <u>The Devil's Dictionary</u>

THIS TALE WAS TOLD to me by my father. The incident did happen; but, time and retelling have embellished it beyond truth. Call it fiction.

Back in the good-ol'-days (1915-1920) there was a plague of ticks in the Southeastern United States. The blood sucking insects concentrated in the cattle population, causing anemia and other related diseases. Many cattle died; a disaster was imminent.

And so it came to pass that the government created <u>The Tick Eradication Bureau.</u> There was the usual flood of red tape. When condensed, the law decreed that all cattle owners were to immerse (dip) all cattle in a mixture of water and emulsified creosote (stockdip) twice each summer. The law also provided a stiff fine and/or imprisonment for those that failed to comply.

The legislators, lawyers, and printers had the easy part.

The agents that were to implement the program in the hills and hollows of Appalachia would have a much more difficult assignment.

Resistance to authority was a way of life in some areas of the Southeast; this was especially true in Appalachia. Europe had disgorged its rebels, misfits, and other human debris on the shores of Appalachia for decades. This imported defiance was further enhanced by the circumstance of history. "Cousins" of the Indian Nations remembered "The Trail of Tears." The Civil War's Confederate veterans still lived, and many retained the attitude of, "Hell, no, we ain't forgittin'." Many more vividly remembered the reconstruction period and its political struggles. Added to this "mix" was the constant war with federal revenue agents by the "white lightening" manufacturers. And then, there were the now free Africans, ex-slaves still remembering the legacy of governmental sanctioned slavery. An attitude of purposeful resentment and rebellion ran rampant in the minds and hot-blood of the natives. It was an ingrained habit.

The open-range for cattle still existed and most herds were as wild and spooky as "hootie" owls. An old matriarchal bell-cow led most herds with a tinkling, clanging bell. This sound became a herd focus and also a guide for the owner when he searched for the herd to dole out salt or special feed. The cattle could be corralled by luring or baiting the old cow and her followers into an enclosure. Dipping all those wild cattle would require patience, diplomacy, and perseverance. Neither man, nor beast would voluntarily submit.

A Good-Ol'-Boy from the county courthouse crowd came to the community and explained the program. He also had the authority and the funds to commission the construction of the dippin' center. Activities at the center would evolve around the concrete dipping vat built below ground level. The dimensions were: 20 ft. long, 3½ ft. wide, 8 ft. deep, with an entrance ramp 10 ft. long, slanted at a 45 degree angle so as to slide the cattle into the vat. Also added was an exit ramp at a 60 degree angle with steps leading out and a concrete drainage apron to catch drippings from the dipped cattle. A walkway ran the length of the vat so that the guideman could prod the cattle to the exit steps and onto the drainage apron.

When the center was complete, the vat was filled with pond water and the prescribed stock dip. (The cattle would later add urine, manure, ticks, lice, flies, mites, and other debris; the men all used tobacco - chewed, smoked, and dipped. The contents of the vat was a potent mixture that became stronger with heat, time, and more cattle.) The Good-Ol'-Boy posted a schedule, sharpened his pencil, set his clipboard on a handy box, and waited expectantly for the herd-of-the-day to appear.

At first it was easy. All went well. The bell-cow led the herd into the corral. The gates were closed and soon the crowding chute bulged with bellowing cattle. The routine was simple: Slide a cow down the ramp - splash - swim her to the exit - give her time to drain - check her off on the clipboard - yell, "Next!", and so it progressed, over and over. It was pleasant. The smell of the cattle, the aroma of the creosote, fresh pine scented air from the mountains, the good humor of the Good-Ol'-Boy almost made it idealistic. There was no hint of the trouble to come.

But one morning, the scheduled herd did not appear. The Good-Ol'-Boy cranked his Model T and drove to the delinquent owner's home, where the owner explained that he was, "Not ready, yet." A copy of the law was produced and read, then reread. But the owner explained, again, that he was, "Not ready, yet." The Good-Ol'-Boy then reread, requested, entreated, supplicated, beseeched, cajoled, and finally begged, and pleaded. "I'm not ready, yet," was still the answer and end result of his diplomacy; so he left in exasperation.

(The malodorous mixture in the vat bubbled, brewed, and bided its' time.)

Three days later, a brand new Ford Model T, four door touring car chugged up to the dipping center. A portly gentleman heaved himself out and onto feet that were clad in new shoes. His suit was also obviously new and a Derby hat, the exact same color as his suit, sat squarely on his round head. A gold chain rested over his ample stomach; and a long, black Havana cigar protruded straight before him. His halo of importance glowed strong enough to cast a shadow behind the local folks that had gathered. He studiously ignored them, surveyed his surroundings, strode to the corral near the vat, and posted a new schedule. Then he addressed the gathering group: "I am Mr. Lubrioson; my first name is Metra and I am the new dipping agent. Only half the cattle have been dipped and my job is to see that the undipped are dipped. There is a new schedule and the notices are in the mail." He pulled a new gold watch from his vest pocket and held it above his Derby hat, "I'll be back at ten o'clock tomorrow morning," he proclaimed. Then he started the new Ford with one pull of the crank and putt-putted away.

There were no cattle in the corral the next day when Mr. Metra Lubrioson returned, accompanied by the sheriff. The schedule was consulted and the sheriff went to the home of the delinquent farmer and arrested him. Due process, before the judge, shortly saw him fined and warned that a jail sentence awaited him if he did not comply with the law.

The cattle were waiting when Mr. Lubrioson returned the next morning. He changed into coveralls and boots, lit his cigar, set up his bookkeeping equipment, and signaled to start dipping. (His hip pocket sagged in such a way that all knew that he was toting a pistol.)

Finally, there was one animal left. It was a huge, black, long-horned bull with an attitude of hell and destruction. Alone, he continued to elude the catch chute and was prepared to continue the contest as long as necessary. However, he was eventually stampeded, bellowing, pawing, and bawling, into the chute. It was there that he hooked his horn behind a post, set his feet and balked. No force could move him. It was the immovable object about to meet the irresistible force.

It was late. Mr. Lubrioson, sweaty, tired, dusty, hungry, and wanting to leave the presence of the slow, dumb, local folks volunteered, "If you'll move out of my way. I'll show you how to put that damn bull into the vat." They obliged.

He clambered into the chute, cigar and all. He then backed away, about ten feet, and charged at the bull's rump. The bull noted his new antagonist, his coveralls, his size, his cigar smoke, his aggressiveness; and the bull, in fear (or revenge) became incontinent and also ceased resisting. Mr. Lubroison smashed into the rump with its new green exudation and the man and animal skidded down the manure lubricated ramp, creating the most awesome splash of the day. When the roiling turmoil abated, Mr. Lubrioson emerged at the exit ramp, holding firmly to the bull's tail. Man and animal paused for assessment after they clambered out. When the bull became aware of the man grasping his tail, he bellowed, whirled, and charged. Mr. Lubrioson dodged, slipped, fell and rolled under the lower planks of the corral into the dirt of the adjoining road. He was uninjured; but his accumulations had made him the filthiest human ever seen in the community. The dirt had coated his coveralls and rapidly became green mud. As he wiped his eyes clear enough to see, the farmer he had had arrested the day before grinned - or was it a smile? - maybe a simper? Anyway, Mr. Lubrioson saw it and rage inflamed him. He clawed the revolver from his filth-filled hip pocket; slung the slime from the barrel and threatened that he would shoot any - any! - son-of-a-bitch that laughed. No one - no one - changed expression. The soggy, muddy coveralls were peeled from his body, as he changed the gun from one hand to the other. He threw the coveralls into the road alongside his boots and walked gingerly to his new Model T touring car wearing only his B.V.D.'s (now green). One pull of the crank and he putt-putted away, never to return to the hollow. Later, it was reported that he was seen wallowing in the water under Cane Creek bridge.

The dipping crew and by-standers stood frozen by the threat. There was no visible reaction; no one would have wished such a dunking on a fellow human. They stood in grave consideration and reconsideration. It was then that the hickory sapling Grandpa was leaning against, began shaking. Grandpa was unable to maintain his silent mirth. A sound resembling a convulsive giggle escaped him. Or was it flatulence? "Laugh and the world laughs with you" proved to be true. The farmer that had been arrested slapped his side and guffawed. A burly youth pantomimed Mr. Lubrioson's plunge. Soon there was breath stealing, side splitting, stomach heaving, convulsive weeping, gleeful, sorrowful, ridiculous and all other versions of laughter. One man was rolling on the ground, another man lay on his back writhing as though caught in a paroxysm.

Some witnesses and participants claim that the merriment lasted an hour; others say a day - or week - because of the glee it reinspired with each new telling.

Versions of this story have been recited over and over. It has acquired a life of its own and is probably all a gross exaggeration. One recitation evokes Divine Providence and the scripture, "Vengeance is Mine saithe the Lord."

Anyway, the farmer that had been arrested became a "True Believer," and others were persuaded that they had witnessed a genuine mystical happening - a rapture.

The Cornfield Mutiny

*Fond memory brings the light
of other days around me
the Smiles, the Tears
of Boyhood years*
                      Thomas Moore (Irish poet)

MEMORY FADES and is refocused by the flow of time. We see the past "as through a glass darkly." The events of this story did occur. The people did, and some do exist, but all differently from my telling.

- - -

It was June of 1928. The cotton and corn had been planted and had germinated to a stand. It was now time to hoe the weeds and grass from the rows and space the plants. Cotton was the cash crop. It paid the mortgage and bought essentials; so the main hoeing crew worked it first. A week or more was required before it would be finished and time allotted to the corn.

My father was impatient to get to the corn before weeds

and grass were out of control. Since no grown-ups were available, he drafted five boys: Harry, Hugh, Herb, H.H., and me. We were cousins, aged eight to eleven. My grandfather laughingly referred to us as "The Gang."

My Grandfather was a genuine frontiersman. He had participated in the Oklahoma land rush of 1889 as a "Sooner." When the excitement had abated he had returned to Alabama only to travel again. This time he had "settled" for three years in Texas with kinsmen of an older sister. A typhoid epidemic had decimated the family and he again returned to Alabama.

He was married, farmed for several years, and when there were five children, he decided to move West. This time he traveled in Oklahoma and Texas visiting old friends and kinsmen in a quest for a place to "settle down." He never found it. When he returned, his wife who became my grandmother accused him of "Lookin' for the end of the rainbow."

On one occasion, he faced down a lynching party with a double barreled shot-gun and simple arithmetic. He said the death of two or more of them was probably a higher price than they wished to pay. They agreed.

The Dalton Gang was active and the James Gang was heroic to Southerners when he went west. His reference to us as "The Gang" was probably an outgrowth of his experience. Also, he developed a dispassionate view of human frailty that served "The Gang" well - as you will see.

"The Gang" was issued five hoes, a file to sharpen them, and an oaken keg of water. We were instructed to go thin the corn and cut the weeds and grass. Ol' Collie, our watchdog, usually accompanied us - especially when we went swimming - but that day, he noted the hoes on our shoulders, sniffed the air, and returned to the shade at the north end of the back porch.

As we trudged to the cornfield, Harry reminded us that we had gone swimming every day for the past week and that it'd be a shame to break a good habit. Visions of the cool water of Thompson's spring gurgling from the limestone bluff and into Mulberry Creek's best swimming hole gave us a sense of pleasure that is describable only to those with similar experience.

We dutifully arrived at the cornfield, stuck the file into a fence post and covered the keg with grass to maintain coolness.

"The Gang" started hoeing and worked steadily for an hour. The sun's rays were relentless, the insects were persistent, and we sweated. Our thirst increased until the attraction of the grass-covered keg was irresistible. We returned to it, slaked our thirst, rested a bit, and then resumed work.

The first set of rows was finished by mid-morning, thus leaving us a half mile from our keg and file. H. H. shouldered his hoe, announced that he had to have a drink and started walking. The usual procedure would have been to hoe back to the keg, but we were also thirsty so we followed. The seeds of mutiny were sown.

Each had a turn at the keg. We rested, sharpened our hoes, rested again, and passed the keg once more. Little Hugh drained it before the second turn was completed and set the keg back onto the grass.

Hoeing was methodically resumed. It was hotter, with the temperatures well into the nineties. Our shirts were soaked. Rivulets of sweat ran down our legs, combined with the dust and became mud on our feet and ankles. Sweat bees, mosquitoes, and assorted gnats swarmed over us.

Harry noticed that his feet and ankles were not being stung or bitten. He also recalled that he had read that elephants covered themselves with dust and mud to ward off insects. Within seconds, his face, arms, and neck were coated. He obtained instant relief.

"We weren't no dummies." Immediately we followed his example and also, for good measure, directed a barrage of dust at the insects, who retreated to the shade of a nearby fence-row to await developments.

"The Gang" congratulated itself and continued hoeing, until someone noted the red-clay coloring of our faces and bodies. One war whoop and we became Indians on the war path. The last Tom Mix picture show was an inspiration. A circle was formed and dancing and prancing began. Our hoes became spears and our straw hats, shields, as two imaginary enemies were slain and scalped.

Trouble was, it was hot! The dust was insulation as well as insect repellant. Our bodies responded by pouring out more sweat as well as perspiration. This double source of moisture was our undoing. The dust became mud; the mud turned into a red ooze; and the ooze melted into salty red paint, salty and flowing red paint. Herb's eyes were the first to be cauterized. His agony became epidemic. Our hands and sleeves were saturated with the ooze mixture; so attempts to wipe our eyes made a bad situation worse.

Proud Indians had become whimpering little wretches in the blinking of an eye.

No one admitted saying it, but the words, "Swimming hole," were heard. Hoes discarded, the stampede started. Our bare feet knew no pain. Briars, brambles, boulders, and brush were ignored. Later, H. H. made the preposterous claim that his feet never touched the ground except when his flight needed guidance.

H. H. was the first to arrive at the swimming hole. As he stopped to remove his clothing, Herb flew by and leaped, fully clothed, into the *coooolll* water, the clear water, the sparklin' water. "We weren't no dummies," the rest of "The Gang" followed Herb's example, rapidly muddying the water with our mud, sweat and crud.

The splashing soon abated and one-by-one we climbed out, undressed and hung our clothing on tree limbs to dry. "The Gang" then returned to the cleansing, the *cooooll*, the restful water for serious swimming and soaking. It was an oasis; it was balm; it was refreshing; it was seductive and could not be denied. We lingered and lingered.

H. H. reminded us that a "thrashin' was a thrashin'," and a minor offense or a major received similar punishment. So our wrong doing was relegated to the back of our minds and we swam some more.

Suddenly, I sensed a change and looked up. There stood our grandfather smiling down on us. The way he was resting against a tree, with Ol' Collie asleep at his feet, made me realize that he had been there for some time.

He explained that we had not responded to the dinner bell and anxious mothers had sent him to investigate. Our trail of discarded straw hats had led him to us. As we walked home, he heard our complaint and explanation. When we arrived, he spoke briefly to my father, who told us to get our hoes and keg and take the remainder of the day off.

Next day, my father accompanied us to the field. A new routine let us stop work in the hottest part of the day and, in three days, the cornfield was free of weeds.

Six decades and more have passed since the mutiny and memory sheds some light on the lives of "The Gang." We were the "baby boomers" following World War I. The rural South has changed drastically since those days. We ignored the depression of the thirties because it made no change in our way of life. Each rural family had a cow for milk and butter, a few pigs for meat and lard, poultry for eggs and fried chicken dinners, tools for repair of clothing, and shelter and an inborn instinct for survival. In short we had the basic necessities. Above all we had the nurture of close kin and friends.

"The Gang" was graduated from the local high school, and a few had attended a year or more of college when World War II began. We all went into the armed services.

Harry became a bomber pilot and fought in both the European and Pacific theaters. He remained, after the war, as a career man in the services and lived in Germany and Japan at various times. He is now retired and operates a hardware store in Hawaii.

Hugh, the youngest, went into the army early and was fatally shot by a Japanese sniper in the Philippines. He died at age twenty-two.

Herb worked for the railway in 1941. He became an engineer and was drafted into the Army in 1942. In 1943 and 1944 he served as an engineer for the Army supply in Europe. After the war he returned to the railway, was married, raised a family and was exposed to smoke. He died in his fifties from lung cancer.

    H. H. went into the infantry. His tank battalion fought in North Africa and Italy, where he was wounded. He was mustered out early with more than the necessary points and a Purple Heart. He was married in North Carolina and moved there. A cousin recently reported that he was alive and well.

    I became a control-tower operator with the Ninth Army Air Force in England and France. After the surrender of Germany, my squadron was scheduled to transfer to the Pacific for the invasion of Japan. I was given leave and had stopped over in Alabama when the nuclear bombs were dropped on Hiroshima and Nagasaki. I felt nothing but relief and happiness. I returned to the farm, was married, and am now retired.

    My grandfather became diabetic, was hospitalized and died from insulin shock. (God, how he loved sweets.) Sometimes I see him in the smiles and gestures of his great-great-grandchildren. Sometimes, I see him looking directly at me when I shave. Sometimes when there is a rainbow in June I see him as through a through a glass clearly.

A Dog Tale - or - A Tale Told by a Wag

THIS STORY IS TRUE. Names and time are changed in case someone that participated in it might be offended. It may be labeled as either fact or fiction. It is a lot of both.

- - -

It was almost the worst of times, January of 1932. A hard freeze had caused ice crystals to spew from the red clay banks of gullies, and mud had remained frozen in the dirt roads. Someone reported that the Coca Cola thermometer at Boss Kelly's store read ten degrees. It was not a fit day for man or beast.

Rural Alabama was experiencing its deepest depression since the Civil War. Cotton bales sat in farmer's yards because there were no buyers. Children wrapped feet in burlap with baling wire as shoe substitutes. Old cotton picking sacks were used as quilts, and underwear and shirts were sewn from feed and fertilizer sacking. Misery was rampant.

The lessons learned in the aftermath of the Civil War were remembered and taught by the old folks. Life went on.

The industrial revolution had almost ended in Metro America and the sons and daughters of the South were returning home, some as sharecroppers. The amenities of rural Alabama were more attractive than a soup line in Detroit City.

And so it came about that Lum Lankey, his wife Lois, and his dog, King moved onto our farm at mid-afternoon on a Saturday in January. The borrowed two-mule wagon contained all their possessions.

The Lankeys unloaded in twenty minutes into a tar-paper shack that had no heat, no electricity, no running water, no insulation - but still better than no house. A fire was started and the Lankeys became a member of our farm community.

In the meantime, the dog King, had explored the adjoining yards, fought and whipped two large hounds and was already marking trees in his new domain. The other dogs, being of sound mind had given tail-wagging obeisance. Our dogs, Ol' Collie and Fritz, had elected to remain under the back porch. King had established his sovereignty in less than one hour.

King was unusual. His ancestry, pit bull and coon hound, had been refined and toughened from years on the American frontier. King was a lean, mean, fighting machine.

At dusk, the Lankeys discovered that the kerosene had spilled from their lamp. Lum, with can in hand, walked across the peach orchard to borrow. King came along to explore more of his new territory. The peach trees required several marking stops and caused King to fall behind his owner. This brought about his fall as Dogdom's leading canine, his ruin.

- - -

I must digress at this point so as to explain what happened a minute later:

My father, a survivor and innovator, had converted an

old cistern in our back yard into a silo. Conversion had required removal of the constricted top and extension of the main body straight up until it was four feet above ground. The resulting structure was a huge brick-and-concrete barrel thirty feet deep and twenty-five feet in diameter. When empty, as it was, it made a big hole in our back-yard. The brick wall above ground was incorporated into our backyard fence. A self-closing gate was convenient to the path across the orchard. The approach from the orchard side gave the impression that the brick wall was just more backyard fence.

King followed his owner to the gate, which slammed shut in his face. Enraged he circled back to do one more tree and noticed the low brick wall incorporated into the fence. His coonhound heritage came to the forefront: Two bounds and he was airborne in exultation and majestic glory. He cleared the wall with two feet to spare.

Then came cold realization:

King saw blackness leading into the bowels of the earth. There was endless falling and terror - regret and dread - and more falling and terror. His howl and scream echo down through the years. The sound was new to all that heard it, including King. It came from him, but in reality it was his ancestry, his genes - his D.N.A. - protesting down through the eons. We kids heard it and required no interpretation. Our genes responded. It was the sound of pure despair, desolation and death.

AAAAHHHHHHHUEWOOOOHHHOOAH!

It was then that Lum knocked on our door. We reluctantly opened the door in fear and received an explanation. Rope and light effected a rescue. King had landed in bilge water and was physically unhurt. Dog and master soon returned home.

King was not seen for three days. Then he returned to dog society as its most peaceful member. Ol' Collie resumed his role as head dog and King became his most subservient subject.

This tale needs an ending! So remember: If you wish to

experience pure despair, desolation, and death, be sure to leap before you look. Also, insure yourself from a fall - never be prideful.

The End of Summer

Hot weather had continued well past the middle of September. It was especially hot around the courthouse square where the draftees had gathered for the long bus ride to Maxwell Army Air Force Base. Departure, scheduled for five a.m., had been delayed because two men were missing. Gertrude, the draft board clerk, suggested a short delay because, as she said, "They may be late 'cause they can't help it."

But, finally she had given up, marked them off the list and told us to "Load up." As we shuffled aboard, an old Plymouth taxi stopped behind the bus and two drunks staggered from it. Names were confirmed and they swayed aboard, flopped into seats, and promptly fell asleep.

All of us had received the official letter that began, "Greetings: You have been selected ...." The intervening three weeks gave us time to make preparation for our adventure. In ignorance we thought ourselves ready for anything that might come our way.

Final good-byes were said through the bus windows. Gertrude delivered the necessary records to an older man and instructed us, "Mr. Bostick is appointed as sergeant in charge until you reach Maxwell. Mind him."

It was a long, hot, loud, and uncomfortable ride in the old un-air-conditioned vehicle. The drunks awoke and shared their bottle, then bought another at a rest stop and also passed it around. Noise continued the entire day as drunken draftees reveled in their new role as unfettered, foot-loose U.S. soldiers.

The heat increased as the day went on. At Maxwell, the muggy hot air was oppressive as we unloaded. Our drunks wilted onto their luggage and did not respond when a career sergeant welcomed us with an open mouth. "Fall in!" he yelled as we milled about in confusion. "You stupid @?*# S$*O@B's" get the hell in line and follow me,' he finally bellowed.

At our mess hall destination, he yelled, "Halt - Stop!", walked down the line, and gave a welcoming speech. "You are now in the Army; when you boarded that bus you became U.S. property. The Army now owns you, body and soul. I am the Army at the present time and you will do as I tell you. Now shut your damn mouths and listen!" he concluded in a rising roar.

His speech was the first step in our transformation into soldiers.

Next day, the men whose last names began with letters "A" through "K" left early. We that remained boarded a bus that went east. The influence of our first day's training was evident as we rode in quiet, subdued wariness. An accompanying sergeant answered all our questions tersely and truthfully. "How in hell do you think *I* should know?" he said.

Raw, new, bewildered, "discombobulated" men crowded the parking/unloading area at Fort McPherson. Confusion reigned - or so it appeared, until someone in uniform held up his hands for "Quiet," and instructed, "Fall in." An amazing thing happened. Groups formed lines with some semblance of neatness and stood expectantly awaiting more instruction.

An organized transformation had begun that would change us into soldiers. We would never be the same again.

Barracks and bunks were assigned with orders to bathe, shave and be ready to 'fall out' again at 1500 hours. Someone explained military time to us and we were ready, as instructed at 3:00 p.m.

The barber shop was more like a shearing shed where skilled "shearers" mowed the hair from our heads in two minutes flat. (The same hair that Joe, our hometown barber had carefully trimmed a few days before for a half-hour.) Uniforms were issued at the Quartermaster, and fitted individually by "guesstimation." A return to barracks for thirty minutes witnessed a change to khaki and finally, we emerged as real uniformed soldiers.

It was only 1700 hours as the warm September sun held onto the day. The war would not wait. Time could not be wasted; so, the medical personnel made preparation for one more group in the physical examination auditorium.

Inside, we were instructed to remove our clothes, place

them in piles, line up in alphabetical order and come forward as our names were called. The process was in reality a gauntlet that moved us from one test to the next. In our paranoia, we shrank from the dozens of prying eyes. Nothing was private ever again: We coughed, breathed deeply, stepped up and down, AAAHHHHED with open mouths, opened and closed eyes, listened to a tuning fork, leaned over, lifted a weight, turned in a circle, urinated in a bottle, bared our veins for drawing blood, and finally finished phase I.

Phase II was verbal: Ever had malaria? Ever had V.D.? Ever been in a hospital? If so, why? Ever broken any bones? Measles? Mumps? Etc.? Etc.?

What grade did you complete in school? Any college? Vocational training? Driving record? Flying experience? Bulldozer experience? Civilian work? Foreign languages? Where have you traveled? Etc.? Etc.?

Most of the time we stood naked, waiting. For all, this was a new experience. Especially new to those that had led a more protected life. Even we with exposure at the old swimming hole were uncomfortable before so many eyes.

Sleep and rest finally came after 2200 hours, and we slept well in the muggy heat of the sun-seared barracks. Complete exhaustion makes sleep come easily under any condition.

Mental testing proceeded the next day to determine alertness, reasoning power, levels of education, and special abilities. After an early noonday meal, lectures were heard explaining our new life as soldiers. These were short talks about: Discipline, protocol, insignia, chain of command, marching orders, uniforms, barracks, personal hygiene, and other information we were to learn before our transformation into soldiers.

Late on the third day, the dreaded vaccinations began. Records show that I was given three shots of my series that first day. (Later, during my three years in the Army, I received vaccinations for typhoid, small-pox, yellow fever, typhus, tetanus, cholera, and two unexplained shots.) On that first day I walked into the hot Georgia sun and blacked out. It was a new experience and as I regained consciousness from an ammonia sniffer I fully realized I no longer controlled my life.

As we progressed from one group to the next, friends went their separate ways and even casual acquaintances were no longer around. A soldier is inevitably cycled into new groups as basic training takes place making the army a lonely place until one learns to acquire new friends after each move. That lesson is one redeeming feature of the military life.

By the fifth day, we thought of ourselves as veterans able to take anything in stride. That's when we loaded onto a troop train, destination unknown. The sun set to our right indicating that we were southbound. Our direction was confirmed late that night as we slumped wide awake in the old coach seats. The train slowed and we saw "St. Augustine" on a depot's side wharf.

The following day at mid-afternoon we marched into Miami Beach and entered a large fashionable hotel. It was to be our basic training post. Excitement ran through the group. There might be sand, swimming, sun, the good life - and even girls! Or so we thought.

Instead, we marched, attended training lectures, ran obstacle courses, marched, shot the M-1 rifle, cleaned the hotel, marched, ate skimpy meals, complained, marched, sang as we marched, double-timed (ran), did K.P. for a full day, marched and became soldiers.

The songs: Caisson's Song, Six Pence, Clementine, Workin' on the Railroad and others are indelibly written on my memory. If the need arises, I can also still respond to marching commands. But our stay in the warm balmy Florida sun came to an end.

The same old passenger day coaches were boarded again and our route was retraced to the north. The uniforms of cotton khaki became uncomfortably cold at night after the first day's travel. By the third day, as we crossed Tennessee, snow could be seen on the shady side of the tracks and at nightfall flurries appeared against the lights of passing towns. Cold air seeped through cracks around windows and someone reported that ice was in the toilet.

We dressed in all our extra clothing and used raincoats as quilts with barracks bags underneath as bedding. The cold increased through the night until hands and feet were numb. A few dozed in the cold but were awakened when the train stopped early the next morning. Snow could be seen across a corn field, with the lights of what appeared to be a small town beyond. Swirls of wind-blown snow beat against the windows and swayed the old coaches as we sat huddled in the cold. Even if we had had woolen uniforms, three days were not long enough to become acclimated to such cold.

Just before daybreak, shouting was heard outside. "Open the doors and fall out!" was commanded in a muffled voice. Men bundled in woolens with ear muffs, galoshes, fur caps, and gloves stood in the snow with flashlights and motioned us out.

Three months training had not been wasted. With numb feet and hands, an orderly exit was managed. A kindly officer took note of our inadequate dress and promptly marched us across the cornfield to a warm auditorium.

Scott Field's Radio Operation and Mechanic school in Illinois received us four days before Christmas in 1943.

No time was wasted after we shuffled cold and weary into the auditorium. Within the hour, barracks and bunks were assigned. An accommodating mess hall prepared a special breakfast and we ate like starved soldiers.

Woolen uniforms with all the cold protecting accessories were issued following the breakfast. Time was allotted to change into the new woolens after a hot shower and a shave.

At 1700 hours a special lecture was scheduled at which a veteran combat flyer explained, in graphic and explicit detail, what the war was about. The only survivor of his bomber crew, he knew his subject firsthand. He began his talk with the words, "Sherman was right. War is hell," and then went on to assure us that as radio operators on bombers, few of us would escape enemy fire. "Half of you will probably be casualties before the year is out," he predicted. "Training, however, can make a difference, so train as though your life depends upon it, because it does," he concluded.

The cold wind seared our faces and brought tears to our eyes as we trudged back to our barracks. Christmas was four days off and our homefolk didn't even know where we were. The season of peace on Earth and goodwill to men seemed to belong to another world - a world outside our time and place.

We quietly walked into the warm barracks, undressed and slid under the woolen blankets. Weariness to the point of exhaustion kept us awake as we reflected on the events that had brought us to this brutal encounter with the cold.

Someone unpacked a small radio and tuned to station KMOX. Bing sang a medley of Christmas songs that ended with "I'll Be Home for Christmas." We shivered in the warmth of our bunks.

Winter came so abruptly at the end of summer.

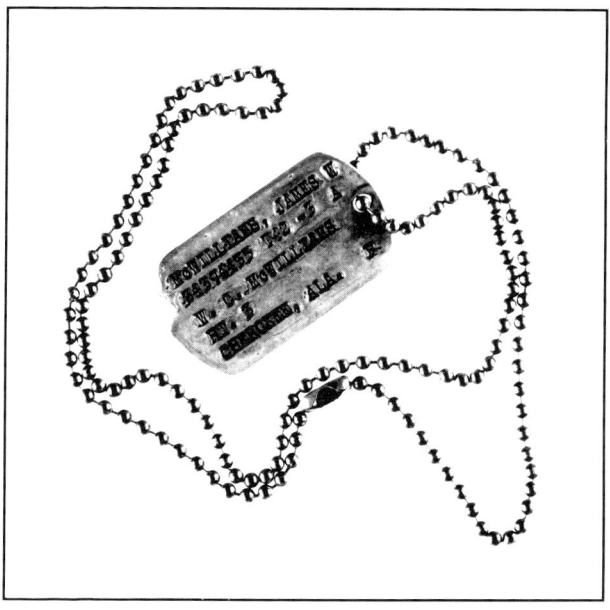

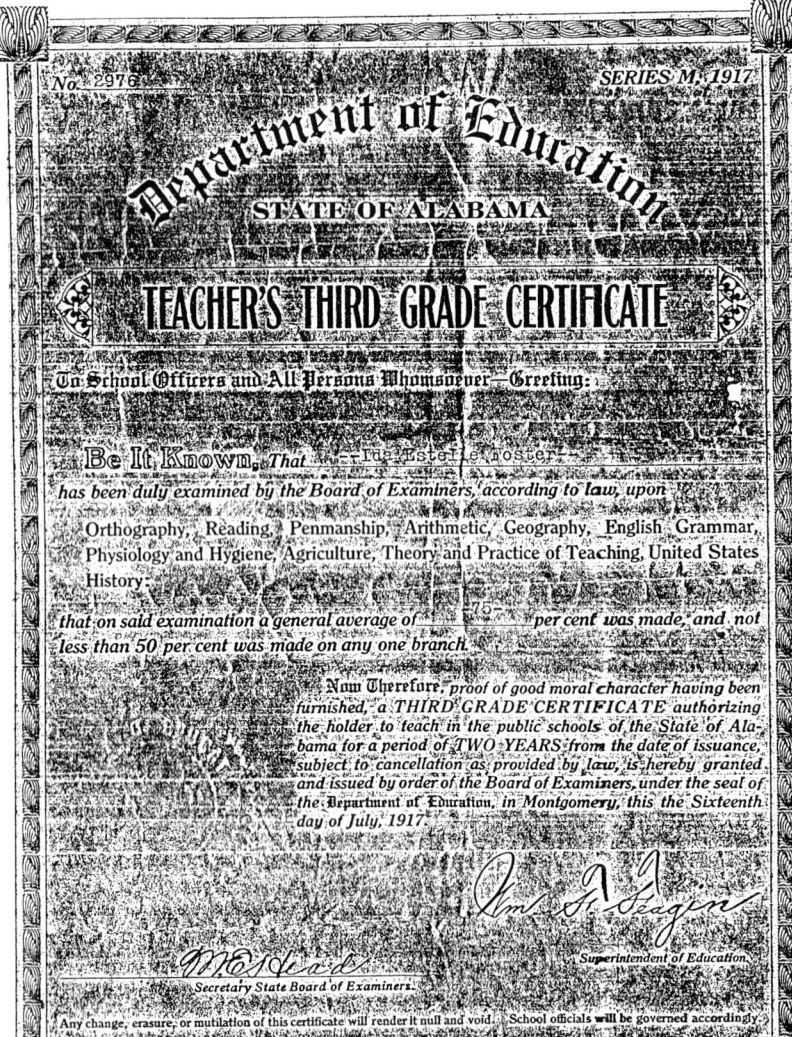

No. 2976 SERIES M. 1917

Department of Education
STATE OF ALABAMA

TEACHER'S THIRD GRADE CERTIFICATE

To School Officers and All Persons Whomsoever—Greeting:

Be It Known, That _____ Ira Estelle Foster _____ has been duly examined by the Board of Examiners, according to law, upon Orthography, Reading, Penmanship, Arithmetic, Geography, English Grammar, Physiology and Hygiene, Agriculture, Theory and Practice of Teaching, United States History; that on said examination a general average of _____ per cent was made, and not less than 50 per cent was made on any one branch.

Now Therefore, proof of good moral character having been furnished, a THIRD GRADE CERTIFICATE authorizing the holder to teach in the public schools of the State of Alabama for a period of TWO YEARS from the date of issuance, subject to cancellation as provided by law, is hereby granted and issued by order of the Board of Examiners, under the seal of the Department of Education, in Montgomery, this the Sixteenth day of July, 1917.

_____
Superintendent of Education

_____
Secretary State Board of Examiners

Any change, erasure, or mutilation of this certificate will render it null and void. School officials will be governed accordingly.

Readin', Ritin' and 'Rithmetic

WE REMEMBER THE HAPPY TIMES and tend to forget the unhappy ones. It has something to do with survival. We are seldom as happy or as unhappy as we imagine. My memory of schooldays in the 1920s is a happy one. My recall is flawed. But read on.

Life in the hollows of Appalachia in those days was a frontier type of existence. Education, of necessity, was fitted to the environment. The varied origin of the people was attested to by their names. A typical listing would be: DuBois, Murphy, Hawk, Rivers, McVay, Kuykendahl, Hovator, O'Malley, LeFevre, and even Marengo.

Semi-isolation had partially preserved speech patterns of the old world. The strong "R" of the Scot could still be heard from my grandpa in his pronunciation of "fire" as "far" and "there" as "thar." The lilt of the Irish could be detected in the rapid speech of others. The sharp pronunciation of the Streits and Reichards reflected the change from German to English. Complete absence of the "R" in plantation English was common to our teachers and echoed coastal English and the African. Later, when schools were consolidated, a student identified his geographical origin in the county by his speech pattern.

Roads leading into the hollows were gravel or dirt. They were winding, naturally pleached and pleasant, until it rained. The typical road led by a school, which was usually a wood- framed building of one or two rooms. They sat on pedestals of stone to avoid ground moisture and termites. Large windows provided extra light because there was no effective artificial light available. The blackboard absorbed much natural light and a few innovative teachers used sheeting to counter this effect when the boards were not in use. The outside of the schools were white with a green trim. (I never saw a red schoolhouse.) Inside were rows of desks, a wood box for fuel, and a teacher's table type desk. A water bucket and dipper helped reduce traffic to the outside. If there were no spring, a well and hand pump was provided with the customary watering trough for passing horsemen or cattle. Two outhouses sat out back — at a distance. Most were two-holes, with the customary Sears Roebuck catalog as the only accommodations. The boys' building was to the left while the girls' building was to the right.

The teachers and students did the janitorial work. Wood for fuel was furnished by parents to defray incidental fees. The traffic of play smoothed the grounds and wore down the weeds and grass.

Lunches were packed at home. A fried egg in a biscuit was typical. Sometimes eggs were boiled and packed in a sack with a shaker of salt and a chunk of corn-pone. Family groups occasionally had beans, stew, buttermilk, etc. from fruit jars. A healthy appetite improves the taste of all food. We sometimes saved the wrapping paper for the next day's fare. Remember: paper was scarce and the general store was miles away.

Classes were from the "primer" through the sixth. High-school aspirants went to a boarding school at more populous centers until improved roads and school buses ushered in the consolidated high school.

The early schools bus was a converted truck. Local carpenters built a large wooden box-like body onto the chassis. Doors, also of wood, provided entrance from either end. Sides were open at eye-level with a rolled canvas closure for rain and cold weather. Three benches ran the length of the body: one on each side and one down the center. They were bare boards, often straight from the saw mill. Black was the universal color that matched all trucks. My first bus was a Model T Ford with wooden spoked wheels. Riding in it beat walking any day.

Mule-drawn covered wagons were sometimes used on rainy mornings. I remember clambering into one on a rainy morning in 1926. Older students immediately cautioned me to avoid touching the canvas top because it would disrupt the flow of water and cause a leak.

Teachers were normally two-year graduates of a teachers' college. They boarded with local families until roads and autos improved enough for commuting. Teacher turnover was rapid. Many were married to local men or found better jobs elsewhere. Those that were married and remained in the community created a devoted clientele for the schools.

School opened in late August but closed for cotton picking. Part of September and October were harvesting holidays. Classes resumed in October and continued until plantin' time in late April. A summer session sometimes supplemented a shortened season. (Gasp, Gasp).

Now to the classroom and teaching: Most teaching was by rote. We recited our ABCs, multiplication tables, states and capitols, vowels and consonants, oceans and continents, etc. until we were programmed for life. We repeated our reading until sound and word interlocked. We wrote until it could be read. We sang until we could keep in tune. We "ciphered" until it was accurate. We studied phonics and participated in spelling bees until we could spell. There was always homework, and report cards monitored our progress. Discipline was not questioned and the teacher always had paddling rights. You shaped up or you shipped out by being expelled. History was taught as dogma - American. We never questioned "the book." Washington did cut down the cherry tree, and we - single handedly - had whipped the British with a little help from LaFayette. Few teachers were equipped to teach more.

A textbook entitled <u>Science For Today</u> taught science as certainty. A little meteorology, physics, chemistry, physiology, biology, etc. were included. I remember some of the indoctrination. "Matter can be neither created nor destroyed;" "There is no escaping earth's gravitational field;" "Speed is limited by the sound barrier;" (Even though we knew about rifle bullets.) There was no hint of the scientific discoveries of those years.

A brief mention of classroom environment: All diseases of childhood were endemic to the classroom. Smallpox vaccine was the only vaccine. There were no antibiotics. Few escaped the epidemics of measles, mumps, whooping cough, croup, scarlet fever, etc. Schools closed when the more virulent plagues, such as polio, meningitis and diphtheria, threatened. Malaria was acute: we all had it. Quinine was the universal medicine and my father bought it in bulk and filled our own capsules by "guesstimation." We dutifully swallowed a pill each day during the "skeeter" season. I would add that there is no sickness equal to the nausea and chills of malaria. The technology that controls it was, and is, a blessing we should appreciate.

Cleanliness was taught, but little practiced. An occasional bath on Saturday night, supplemented by daily hand and face washing, was practiced by the more enlightened families. I know, however, that some kids never bathed - until summer. This lack of sanitation was a constant source of infection (and reinfection) by contact parasites and bacteria. Scabies, impetigo, ringworm, pediculosis, boils, and other scourges were indiscriminately bestowed upon all school personnel.

The hollow that I recall had no telephone, electricity, radio, pavement, doctor, store, plumbing, screens, air conditioning, or other modern amenities. It now has all these and more. But there was the advantage of a close-knit community. Everyone knew everyone. There were mutual respect, kindness, and tolerance. Kids received lessons in good manners by example. An affirmative answer to an adult was always, "Yes, Sir," or, "Yes, Ma'am." Excessive provocation was customarily mediated by neighbors. Your livelihood depended on friendly folks around you. No one locked doors at night, even when locks were available. Pilfering was minor when it occurred and was written off as a donation to someone without the manners to ask for it. There was tobacco - used by most grown ups, but kids used it only surreptitiously. Alcohol fit the same pattern; drunkenness was frowned on, but a drink between friends on gala occasions was accepted.

Education was not a monopoly of the school.

The experience of Appalachia was not unique. Pockets of the American frontier remained in many areas. The Ozarks and the Bayou of Louisiana are examples. These areas have produced people of great stoic adaptability. The changes of the past six or seven decades have provided opportunities for them. They and their children are found in the fore-front of American endeavor today. Their disadvantage became an advantage: They lived during extremely perilous and unhappy times and imagined themselves happy.

The Great "Lime" Disaster

OUR DAUGHTERS, ages four and five, burst into the warmth of the kitchen with cries of, "Daddy, Mama, we'll never get it all cleaned and swept." They were obviously disturbed and on the verge of tears.

The events that had led to this disturbing and dismal pronouncement will delight you.

We had mild winters during the late forties and early fifties; and, as a result, our daughters had never seen a snow. We had no television and seldom saw a movie that had snow scenes. They had no second-hand concept of snow. To them it was a make-believe thing that one saw on Christmas cards or heard in songs.

Then, finally, in January, we had a snow! It was cold as kraut that morning so I hurried to finish the farm chores and ran to the warmth of the kitchen with the anticipation of enjoying the magic and excitement of our little girls' first snow.

They were awakened to a breakfast of waffles, sausage, maple syrup, and hot chocolate; but we did not mention the snow. Then we adults sat at the table as our excitement increased. The camera was loaded. The aroma and warmth of the kitchen increased our expectations, and appetites.

Five long expectant minutes later we heard the girls chattering as they approached the kitchen. We were poised in anticipation of their happy reaction to the snow. Imagine our surprise at the frowns of concern as they burst into the kitchen with cries of, "Daddy, Mama, we'll never get it all cleaned and swept."

"Get what swept?," I asked.

"Someone spread lime on everything last night. It's on the front porch and on the car; it's <u>everywhere</u>, we'll never get it all swept away."

Adult ignorance has no limit: We had forgotten that they did not know snow. There was no reason for them to be excited about "snow" because it was an unknown thing.

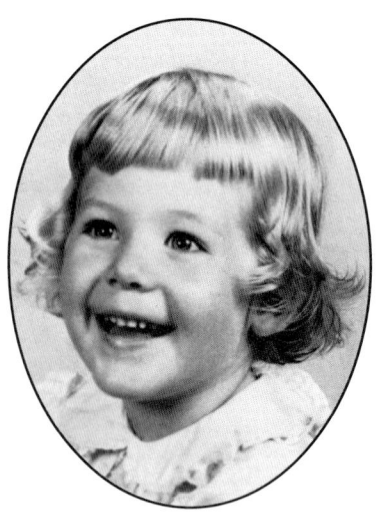 

There was, however, an understanding of a landscape covered with white lime.

You see, the red clay soils of our farm had been "limed" on several occasions because it is required for optimum productivity. The sight of a white landscape could be explained only as lime - whitening to them.

They were coaxed to the front porch and we demonstrated snow to them. They tasted it, rubbed it on rosy cheeks, made it into snowballs, and were chilled by it. We returned to breakfast and the waffles and sausage were consumed with appetites akin to two polar bear cubs. The excitement of snow was building.

An hour later, clad in boots and parkas, two little girls were as experienced in snow as Eskimos. They rolled in it, built two snowmen and even stored a container of snow in the deep freezer for future activities.

The great lime disaster had become the wonderful magic of snow for two little girls.

Eddie Was Not a Coward

Now, the snake was more subtle than any beast.
                                                Genesis 3:1

EDDIE was not a coward. His nose, offset to the right side of his face, attested to his history of valor and his steely ice-blue eyes advertised that he would take no "snuff" from any man.

But he was reduced to a state of "running fit" cowardice by an annoyed, enraged and self-confident black racer snake on a hot day in July of 1929.

If we are to understand Eddie's abnormal behavior, we should know what he had been taught as a child of the rural South. Also, we need a little knowledge of the black racer snake's natural habits.

Mankind has never understood the snake. Because of this they have become man's personification of evil. This has been true since Eve was led astray, and even today, we still speak of the proverbial "snake in the grass." Most kids of Eddie's generation were taught to fear snakes. This fear was imprinted so indelibly that it was not erasable. They were imbued with "snake" fear.

Many snake legends add to this fear: A "hoop" snake will

grasp its tail in its mouth thus becoming a hoop that can roll rapidly in pursuit of its quarry. A poisonous spike on its head can impale its victim who then dies instantly. One snake, supposedly, struck a tree accidentally and killed it, "just like it was struck by lightning."

Another legend claims that a "coach whip" snake wrapped its coils around a man and whipped him viciously until the snake was cut away with a pocket knife.

Still another legend claims that a tooth from a rattlesnake broke off in a shoe. A year later, this tooth scratched a man's ankle and killed him.

Also it is claimed that calves starved when "milk" snakes nursed all the milk from cows resting down by the creek.

It isn't all myth: People do die from snake bites and large snakes do swallow small prey alive. The puff adder does swell to an exaggerated size that frightens people.

And the black racer snake of the Southeastern United States does grow to a more than six foot length. They will run - or charge - at any man. Then, the snake will chase him if he is routed. Large racers sometimes add to the "scare" tactic by lifting their head above the grass in these assaults. The head bobs and weaves in a fearsome grotesque way that discombobulates all but the very brave, or the foolish. Dogs, cattle, wild animals, and people stampede when a large racer charges. But rural boys have been known to play chase with racers; and, I should add, the snake seems to enjoy the play.

- - -

Eddie was a trusted and diligent worker that Dad hired to cut a field of johnson grass hay. When he arrived on that fateful morning, the mules, Sam and Bess, were already hitched to the mower. Eddie tied his water keg to the hames, hung his poke sack lunch under the seat, snapped the reins, and muttered, "Giddiup."

They stopped at the pond for Sam and Bess to tank up on water. Their next stop was in the hay field, where Eddie slid off the seat and placed his keg in a cool shade. He then lowered the sharp blade, remounted, snapped the reins, and repeated, "Giddiup."

Sam and Bess were given free rein and easily navigated through the first round. They then stopped for the customary "breather" while Eddie untwisted a knot of grass from the pitman rod. The usual, "Giddiup" was murmured and they began the second round.

They (Eddie and the mules) did not know about the disturbance they had caused as they passed a large sunning racer snake on their first round. He had glided from his favorite basking spot into the undergrowth of the fence row as they clattered by. The snake had swallowed a young rabbit the night before and only wanted to bask and digest in his favorite sunning spot. After the noise of the mowing had faded, he had crawled back into the open field and found the swath cut by the mower. It was a large sun-filled spot just right for his over six foot length. His second basking was just beginning when he heard the clattering monster approaching again.

(The snake had developed his bluffing and chasing technique for years. He was the very best at intimidation.)

Rage inflamed him and when he sensed the mowing machine's rapid approach, he slithered toward it at full speed like a black streak. As he gained speed, he lifted his head and forward body higher and higher.

When Sam and Bess first saw him, his bobbing head was a good two feet high and moving toward them at breakneck speed. They snorted and lunged toward the open field. Eddie, one of the best mule-skinners, slapped the reins over their backs and firmly pulled them back into line with a loud, "Gee-whoa!"

Sam and Bess balked, just as the snake charged up to them. Momentum carried the snake against the chains, between the mules and the tongue of the mower. The collision never slowed the snake but did help him to mount to the tongue with one long smooth glide.

The snake was then looking down on Eddie!

Only then did Eddie finally realize why Sam and Bess were acting up. The racer snake's precarious balance on the tongue made him appear much larger and the added elevation emphasized the movement of the snake's head. Eddie was terrified, horrified, petrified. Fear engulfed him, as the snake came on down the tongue.

Eddie's steely ice blue eyes glazed over into an awful blankness and he fell from the seat. The snake continued over the seat, over Eddie, into the grass and vanished - his mission completed.

Bess and Sam stood stock still waiting for the "Giddiup" signal. They heard nothing and began grazing as the snake was forgotten.

Eddie, seemingly, had fainted. He lay quivering on the ground. But shortly, his quivering stopped and after a few spasmodic attempts, he jerked himself to his feet and haltingly began running. There was gradual improvement with each step until he speeded up to headlong flight.

When he came into view at the end of the pasture, Dad saw him and later exaggeratedly claimed that Eddie had touched ground at only the high places. Eddie ran past Dad, showing no sign of stopping or slowing. Dad followed yelling, "Stop, Eddie! Eddie, wait! Hold It!" When he finally halted, Dad came up to him and asked, "What's wrong, Eddie?"

Eddie's eyes were unfocused and his breath came in loud gasps, "Snake! Snake! Snake! Snake!," he repeated, piteously pleading between breaths.

A crowd gathered and someone led Eddie to the well and doused him with a bucket of water. The steely blue eyes came into focus, the panting and gasping slowed and Eddie incoherently began explaining what had happened.

This writer was among those that finally understood what had occurred.

And this writer agrees. Eddie was not a coward.

Mamaw's Unfinished Quilts

A rich child often sits in a poor mother's lap.
                              Danish proverb.

AT FIRST, THERE WERE only four of us: There were the little orphans she acquired when she was married to Dad, after our mother's death. After that there were the four of her own to add to the family. Then the eight of us were married and brought grandchildren back home for visits. And in her later years, the grandchildren brought great-grandchildren back home. She always had a new favorite Little One to pamper.

There are more than half a hundred of us now and counting.

She always kept toys in a corner box and her cookie jar had an unending supply of her special "teacakes." No parental protest could overcome the allure of those cakes; sweets were never to be forbidden at Mamaw's. The parent usually relented and munched cakes along with the Little Ones even as they protested.

The Little Ones soon learned to "make a bee line" to Mamaw's cookie jar before parents were aware of their intentions. A "done deal" at the cookie jar was easier than begging dumb parents.

- - -

Quilting bees were an important part of Mamaw's social life. They gave the womenfolk a chance to visit, gossip, report, compare notes, and, in general, to air a woman's viewpoint in a male-dominated world. Above all else, they produced a necessary commodity for the drafty homes of those days. Quilts!

Mamaw became an artist when she quilted and, sometimes, consulted with this writer about colors and patterns. But then, she always did it her way. Quilts, as an art form, had been collector items for years and most homes displayed a collection. They were seen on walls as well as beds, even sometimes, as tablecloths.

The names of various patterns were as colorful as poetry: Wedding Ring, Sunset, Rainbow, Log Cabin, Diamond Square, Map, and Sleeping Kitten were a few examples. Mamaw's artwork was distributed far and wide.

The writer remembers the day she came to us: Dad had brought us home from our long visitations among the kinspeople. We had slept in our own beds again and awoke to the smell of woodsmoke, sausage, and home. The cold in our bedroom had goaded us to dress hurriedly and to rush to the warmth of the kitchen for a breakfast of boiled oats, biscuits, butter, sausage, milk, and hot chocolate. We ate like starved puppies. A dish pan of cold water vibrated on the hot eyes of the old wood-burning cook-stove. Our animated chatter harmonized with the crackling fire. We were happy to be home again.

Then Dad had opened the kitchen door and stood surveying the scene. He announced, "Meet your new Mama; her name is Cora; you may call her Mama Cora, if you like, or just Mama." We saw a pleasant, friendly, young woman and within minutes, we, as individuals were introduced. Before breakfast was over, we had resumed our normal activity. After a few days, "Mama Cora," became "Mama" to us.

It was a name she kept until grandchildren changed it to "Mamaw."

This writer hesitates to credit any specific child with the change and the child's claim to fame. Needless to say, it was appropriate and shortly became her "real" name as though she had never had another.

(Maw was an affectionate title bestowed upon rural mothers in those days; so one of Mamaw's Little Ones combined "Maw" and "Mama" into "Mamaw." For all time to come, she will be remembered as "Mamaw.")

She had grown up in a family with five boys. As a result, she knew how to control boisterous country kids. This writer remembers well the sting of a bitter weed switch on his bottom and legs when he had disobeyed. A family routine was established and maintained. Meals, haircuts, housecleaning, baths, wash day, gardening, study, and all other chores were efficiently done. Remember: This was during the depression years, World War II years, the continuing agricultural recession years, and there was never enough money. However, there was the nurture and care of family. It brought us through sickness, schooling, the war, the depression, teen-age-madness, and finally, perhaps, to maturity. Mamaw was always there for her children and, even when her health declined, her love and resolve continued unabated. She kept us from harm's way.

In her later years, with its many hospitalizations, she became more and more frail, but she always returned home to her quilting and visiting with her Little Ones. She bounced back from sickness using her own therapy. Her memory never failed, but her body became weaker with each new pain.

As time passed, she used a walking stick. Then she needed crutches; and finally, a four-legged walking aid was necessary. A wheelchair was used on occasion, but she scorned it and always preferred the walker. It demonstrated more independence.

The writer can see her now: It is breakfast time and she is shuffling her walker down the hallway toward us. When she sees us waiting there, she warns, "You better get out of the way. The old grey mare is headin' for the feed trough."

or:

She is sitting in the electrically controlled chair that assists her to a standing position: She and the Little Ones are raising and lowering the chair, while she, as Commander, experiments with "the spaceship command module." The Little One is tethered to the cable control switch and will always remember his "space walk with Mamaw."

or:

She is experiencing one of her ornery days: The writer is preparing breakfast; and she, again, reminds him that yesterday's bacon was burnt and the toast was not crisp. And then she continues, "Oats should be stirred until they are firm and well-done; and while you are at it, don't break the yellow of the egg. Fried eggs over medium are not scrambled eggs. I don't want scrambled; I want over medium. If the yolk is messed up it's scrambled. I want fried egg, over medium," and then she continued; "I don't want scrambled eggs."

or:

She is remembering: her memory was almost perfect. Even minute details were vividly recalled and she tells us about Grandpa and the watermelons: Listen: "He hauled four wagon loads of melons with three men helping. They passed them hand to hand into the old moat, through the windows of the basement, and placed them carefully in the cool, dark corners. The melons rode on straw and were not bruised. We ate all we could. We gave some away. We wasted several by eating the heart only. After a week they started rottenin' and stinkin' and then Grandpa and the men toted 'em out in buckets, they was so mushey, and hauled them off again."

or:

She tells about Henry Watkins' accident with the Old Dodge car. Listen again: "Henry washed Ol' Sue; he checked the oil and water; he put the hood down; then he reached through the window and turned the switch on without checking the gear shift. He then cranked Ol' Sue in low gear. The motor caught on the first pull and headed for a brick wall with Henry between the car and the wall. Henry sidestepped, opened the car door and grasped at the gear shift lever just as the car hit the wall. Ol' Sue had a spring bumper that bounced her back when she hit. The force of the impact and the bounce back drove Henry's head through the plate glass windshield and cut his neck bad. Blood was everywhere as he screamed for help. We scooped soot from the chimney and spider webs from the closets and applied the mixture of these to stop the bleeding. Then we tied his shirt around his neck. Dr. Adams said we saved his life."

No one knows how many quilts and quilt tops she made. There were probably more than a hundred. They became collector items of value that she sold at give-away prices of ten to twenty dollars each.

These dollars were salted away in a savings account, with other funds that came her way, and grew to a modest bequest for her children. Mamaw's quilts warm us even now.

And then, one morning she elevated her chair and reached for her walker. Her grip gave way and she fell. It embarrassed her but she insisted, "It didn't hurt much." However, the next day she confessed to more pain and, upon our insistence, she returned to the hospital. Her injury was untreatable because of her age and other conditions.

She reminded us, from her hospital bed, that a few unfinished quilts were in her quilt box and two new Little

Ones had not been brought home for her to hold in her arms. Those were her regrets at age eighty-five.
Mamaw left us three days later ─────────────
───

The two new Little Ones will have no memory of her. A few quilts remain - unfinished.

The Clovis Point

There were giants on the earth in those days.
                                        Genesis 6:4

[atlatl (at'-lat-l) A throwing-stick used to hurl a spear]

YOU COULD ALMOST feel its presence: Bits and pieces of flint had indicated its nearness for years. A broken base piece was found here; then a large chopping type flint was found there. The evidence accumulated until we knew, for certain, that the Clovis People had camped at Hogan's Pond.

And then, finally, I saw it! The base of what seemed to be a perfectly formed Clovis point stuck out of the red clay near a cotton stalk, two rows over.

The hair on my neck moved and I breathed deeply. It was exquisite excitement. One hundred centuries - and more - may have elapsed since human hands had touched it. This marvel of flint art reflected intelligence. A robust people had passed this way.

The hot sun beat down, and I wiped the sweat from my eyes with my sleeve. A second glance confirmed it. There, two cotton rows over, lay a Clovis point. In my hesitation, anticipation and imagination, in my reverie, I heard a wolf-dog's howl and bark. Then the fearsome sound of a saber-toothed tiger's guttural cough and roar was also heard. In my growing fantasy the murmur, the babble of human voices reached my ear from down near Hogan's Pond. The Lu Clan! The Clovis People!

Sometime between two hundred centuries and one hundred centuries ago, the Clovis People - the ancients - had roamed over all of North America. In their migrations they had encountered herds of huge elephant-type hairy mastodons. The saber-toothed tiger, with eight-inch tusks preyed upon large herds of ruminants. The giant cave bear shuffled about. The thousand pound ground sloth waddled under the forest canopy and beavers, as large as hogs, dammed the creeks.

The ice age had ended. But nature's large animals, adapted to the cold, still remained. It was a hunter's paradise, if the hunter were strong, adaptable, and intelligent.

Then in my reverie, I saw Gulu and his younger brother Malu. The two had pursued a young mastodon bull into the water of Hogan's Pond a hundred centuries ago and had lost a Clovis point.

They and their two wolf-dogs carefully crawled upwind to within two man-lengths of the mastodon. The dew-soaked leaves suppressed sound and gave them time to stand and implant two spear projectiles into the animal's rib cage before it became aware of them. The wolf-dogs snapped and bit at its head giving them the opportunity to thrust their large hand-held spears into the vulnerable exposed belly. When the bull, finally, spotted his main attackers, it had loped away with another spear-projectile in its haunch from Gulu's atlatl throwing stick.

The mastodon was a "loner" ostracized from the herd by the dominant male who chased him away before the herd

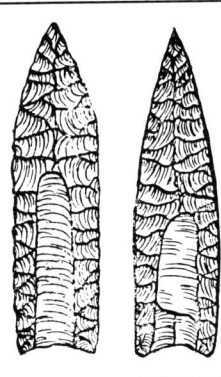

CLOVIS POINT

Medium sized dart point.
Identification; fluted lanceolate point with parallel or slightly convex sides and concave base. Widest point is near middle of blade, flutes vary in length from very short to almost full length of blade. The point usually is rather thick and base may be ground.
Usual size 1½ to 5 inches. Age 20,000 B.C. to 10,000 B.C.
Found over all of North America but very sparsely.

crossed "The River That Runs North" two days before. The huge male then stood guard as the herd forded the river at its nearest downriver shoals. The "loner" crossed a day later.

The Lu Clan had migrated with the mastodon herd for one moon of time so as to be near when the young bulls were abandoned. A mastodon kill would support the Clan for two moons or more.

Gulu, from the Clan's camp upstream, saw the lone young bull as it crossed the river. He and his brother Malu summoned two wolf-dogs and then trailed the young bull. The rest of the Clan was left to feast on mussel meat at the river bank.

At mid-morning they came up to their quarry, grazing in a sunny glade unaware of the men and wolf-dogs. When it had eaten its fill, the young bull flopped in the sun and dozed. It was then that they attacked it.

The blood flow from the wounded bull was enough to assure easy tracking so Malu ran back to the Clan's camp and instructed the thirty members to follow the broken branch trail he and Gulu would make.

He immediately retraced his steps and added more broken branches to Gulu's trail markings. Within three hand widths of sun movement, Malu sensed that Gulu was nearby. The trail of blood was fresher and broken twigs had fresher leaves. A wary approach brought him to a clearing near a large pond where he could see Gulu and the wolf-dogs resting near a huge water-oak tree. Then he saw the mastodon bull belly deep in water about four man-lengths from the pond's edge. The bull was obviously weak and unable to travel farther.

The large low-limbed tree spread protective branches over the area and out to the wounded mastodon. Men and wolf-dogs watched the animal for half a hand width of sun movement. They then cautiously approached, using the tree trunk as a blind, and, simultaneously leaped from opposite sides of the tree and hurled two more atlatl spear projectiles into the animal's chest. Blood blew from its trunk reddening the water, as he roiled about in his death throes. In three howls of a wolf-dog the mastodon fell broadside, kicked about in the frothy bloody water, and died.

The brothers cautiously waded out to their dead quarry and retrieved their spears. Gulu hacked a chunk of meat from the shoulder with his flint knife and tossed it to the hungry wolf-dogs. Two spear points were broken, but with their deer antler chipping tool they rapidly resharpened them to a new point.

As soon as they were rearmed, Malu sloshed back to the mammoth's carcass. He clambered upon it, drew his furs about him with draw strings, and settled into a semi-sleep, taking care to remain upright so as to tumble if he completely dozed off. Gulu swung into the large tree's lower branches, wedged himself next to the main trunk, and slept.

The Clan's trailblazer and the two following guards arrived a few heartbeats before the main clan body. Gulu and Malu received the usual praise for their hunting ability and then the Clan set about preparation for their camp and the night. Wood was scavenged from the surrounding forest, and Falu, the fire maker, created a fire with his fire sticks. Plant bulbs were dug from the pond's banks; edible vegetables were gathered; and, most importantly, the liver and heart were lifted from the giant body after a rib was hacked away.

By sunset the clan feasted on roast mastodon liver, bits of raw heart meat, singed roots, raw bulbs, and tasty leaves of the edible vegetables. The children were doled some honey-comb that one young man, with an eye swollen shut, had robbed from a hollow tree beehive.

Clan leaders knew that the spoor of dead mastodon would attract the carnivores; so they immediately made preparations for the expected onslaught. Extra wood was gathered and piled at the base of the large tree. Access to the lower branches was assured with steps made by tumbling two large boulders against the tree's trunk. Spear and atlatl projectile were inspected. Later, Gulu selected his three most proficient spearmen as night sentinels, who were to alternate watches with him, two at a time so as to assure wakefulness.

The Lu Clan fell asleep in family groups under the leaves they had gathered for insulation. Furs were wrapped closely, as they huddled for warmth between the fires and the base of the tree.

Three hand widths of moon motion later, the two sentinels heard it. A barking howl downwind came from one wolf-dog, warning them of danger. A saber toothed tiger answered with his dreaded guttural coughing roar. The two sentinels leaped into instant action and sounded the danger signal, a staccato night bird call.

Response from the Clan was just as prompt and organized. The women and children clambered into the lower limbs and climbed above the range of a tiger's leap. The men and boys threw more wood onto the fires and then spread the fires before the tree in a semi-circle. Hand spears were given men on the lower limbs and extra atlatl projectiles were arranged for easy access.

Gulu instructed his sentinels to remain with him between the fire and tree. Each was armed with a large hand-spear and three atlatl spear projectiles.

The dogs signaled the approach of the tiger. A few heart beats later his amber eyes and long white saber tusks glowed as he hesitated before the fire. The spoor of the dead mastodon was to the right of the camp and beyond the fires and puny human beings; so the tiger circled to the right in a loping run. This gave each sentinel the best mark with the atlatl projectiles. Four spears protruded from his left side before he came to the water of the pond. The wolf-dogs, emboldened by Clan help, sank teeth into the cat's left haunch and right back leg. The pain from these simultaneous attacks caused him to turn on his tormentors. A swipe from the tiger's front left paw mangled the wolf-dog hanging to his left haunch. Free of the dog, the tiger charged the four men. Gulu thrust his large hand spear into the tiger's broad chest while three more atlatl projectile were hurled into his sides. Gulu was bowled over by the lunge. The tiger was upon him instantly and impaled a six inch saber tooth into his skull. The fang stuck and Gulu's body was flung about in the tiger's attempt to free it. When finally free, the tiger crushed the head of the mauled dog and staggered toward the darkness of the forest, as one more spear, thrown from the tree, pierced his back.

The remaining wolf-dog followed the tiger into the forest. Half a hand of moon motion later the tiger staggered in a half circle, fell, and died with a final bubble of blood from his nose. The wolf-dog signaled the clan with his "victory" howl. He ripped the tiger's liver from the soft under belly, retreated to the underbrush, and ate it. Carnivores from the forest congregated and by morning's light only bones and bits of skin remained of the giant cat.

The Clan had descended from the tree when they heard the victory howl. They rekindled the fires. Malu sat beside Gulu's body in the firelight and chanted the song of "farewell." Gulu's valuable clothing furs were removed and a length of the mastodon's leg skin was fitted over him. Afterwards Malu floated the body to a deeper part of the pond and sank it with a few stones.

When he returned, the family leaders acclaimed him the new Clan chief.

At daybreak Malu signaled the wolf-dog to lead him to the tiger's death site. When there, he recovered a hand fingers count of projectile points and one large spear.

Three points were never recovered a hundred centuries

ago.

    A train whistle, in the distance imitated the howl of a wolf-dog and ended my reverie. The Clovis point still protruded from the red clay, two rows over near a cotton stalk. I retrieved it, brushed it, examined it. It was a perfect Clovis point!
    Two more are out there somewhere.

Maturity?

Some people are molded by their admirations, others by their hostilities.
Elizabeth Bowen - <u>The death of the heart</u> - 1938.

JOHN SAT QUIETLY listening to his grandson venting his anger through the telephone. "If my car isn't ready tomorrow afternoon, I'll have a tow-truck pick it up and take it to another garage," he declared. Then the grandson, Charlie, had added, "I won't pay a cent for any work you've already done on it. It's not my fault that you can't get the repair parts." Charlie slammed the phone down and turned, "Where are the aspirin, Gramps? My head is killing me."

"In the bathroom medicine cabinet," John had answered. Then he continued, "Take it easy, Charlie. You are of more value than the car. Even if you never see the car again, the harm you're doing yourself is more costly than the car's value. Ask a doctor about stress and high blood pressure. Now, do us all a favor; call the man you just chewed out and apologize. Then work out an agreement and apologize again. You'll feel better without having to swallow those aspirins and your car will be repaired sooner."

"But, Gramps, when you're angry you need to get it out of your system. It's "best" to get it out; use that adrenaline before it causes ulcers," Charlie had explained.

"A bad habit is a bad habit is a bad habit," John recited. "Habits build with practice, build with practice, build with practice. If you practice a bad temper, it becomes part of you. Your face reflects it. Your body language indicates it. And your mind harbors hostility. Those that might otherwise be friends become wary at the first sight of you. Think about it and change your attitude. Smile!"

"But I need my car now," Charlie explained, "They promised it today if the parts came in."

"Take my car," John countered. "Drive over to the garage and personally apologize for your outburst; if you want your car repaired on time. Your tantrum has triggered similar feelings in everyone that has heard you or seen you. By now, it has probably influenced a dozen people. Feelings of anger multiply because others reflect emotions. Think about it. Two people heard you. Those two react and meet others who in turn are influenced. It multiplies. A little restraint goes a long way. In our world of rapid communication, one angry man could inflame a majority of the people. Remember Hussein?"

"Gramps, you don't understand," Charlie insisted. "Anger gives us the energy that has helped the race survive. It adds to our strength in a fight. It makes us fearless and brave enough to face a foe. It even insulates us from pain, because in anger, our body ignores pain."

"We don't live in a jungle any more," John reasoned, "Our jungle is different. Reasoned, rational response and restraint is a more fitting reaction to adversity. Anger makes for recklessness, destruction, and wastefulness. Your enemy wants you angry so as to gain an advantage. Remember the old adage, "Whom the gods would destroy, they first make angry." As for pain, it is the body's way of signaling you of danger. If you ignore a pain signal, you ignore your own destruction. Why do you have a headache?"

"Then how am I to relate to all those S.O.B's out there waiting to take advantage of me?" Charlie questioned.

"First things first," John advised. "Maintain your own integrity as much as you can. When you lose your temper, you are just another S.O.B. A clear mind usually has the advantage and can react appropriately. Remember, you don't keep a sinking boat afloat by drilling more holes in its bottom."

"If no one becomes angry, what is to motivate us to correct the wrongs of this world? Who is to speak out? Who will fight evil?" Charlie insisted.

John cautioned, "There are varieties of anger. Conserve your anger and direct it efficiently through reasoned action. Don't waste anger on men, who are only symptoms of stupidity, bad motivation, corruption and other superficial evils. Save your anger. Hoard it for the long haul. Keep it under control for your health's sake. Never indulge in a tantrum because it requires another to keep it company. If you become emotionally angry - and we all do at times - sit quietly until it has passed. Use restraint. The best way to eliminate an enemy is through a kind, quiet, reasoned response."

Charlie appeared to be in deep thought. A smile spread over his youthful face and he reflected, "You know, you may be right, Gramps. I'll start by phoning the garage right now. I'd sure like to eliminate that one S.O.B."

"Yes, give it a try," John ironically replied.

Dad's Old Ledger

That which costs little is less valued.
Cervantes <u>Don Quixote</u> 1605-15

I would rather be able to appreciate things I can not have than to have things I am unable to appreciate -
Elbert Hubbard <u>The Note Book</u> 1927

3/10/40 Delivered - 300 Bales of Hay @ 3¢ per Bale Credited-$9.00
W. C. McWilliams <u>Ledger</u> 1940

THE OLD LEDGER is worn, frayed, dog-eared, with many sheets loose, some missing. "Price-$1.25," was written with a heavy marking pencil, long ago, in the upper left hand corner of the front cover. These covers have a stylized design of squares and triangles in black heavy lines that accent the word, "Ledger," in the exact center of the front cover. Dark maroon colored leatherette triangles encase the rounded corners of the front and back covers. Dust mites, moths, and silverfish have eaten away bits of paper here and there. The refuse from these insects give it a dry, dusty, musty smell.

The old ledger partially records the struggle of the writer's Dad during the years from 1939 - '54. The mind and body ache in empathy and in remembrance.

The depression of the early thirties, supposedly, had run its course, but few farmers had been alerted to this happening. World War II came and went with some improvement, but the necessary changes made unavoidable by the Industrial Revolution still lagged on most farms. A chronic recession held sway out in the country.

The listings, notes, entries and general conditions in agriculture might be of interest to the reader. The writer hopes to convey an insight into those times and events. He did tap emotions he had forgotten to remember and renewed an attachment to his beginning. It was a reawakening of fond memories.

There is no plot. Imagine your own:

- - -

Chick's account (Broiler Chickens)

December 3, 1939 bought 500 baby chicks $60.00
December 23, 1939 bought 300# broiler mash 8.10
December 29, 1939 bought 100# broiler mash 2.70
January 4, 1940 bought 200# broiler mash 5.50
January 9, 1940 bought 6 boxes Walco Tablets 3.00
Etc...   Etc...   Etc...   Etc...<u>Etc...</u>

Total Expenses $299.80

Sold Chicks

February 28, 1940 - 103# @ 20¢ per # - Mason's $20.60
March 1, 1940 - 57# @ 25¢ per # - Mason's 11.40
March 3, 1940 - 16 chicks - Hampton's 9.50
March 5, 1940 - 62# @ 20¢ per # - McCollum's 12.40
Etc...   Etc...   Etc...   Etc...<u>Etc...</u>

Total Receipts $111.20

    Of course, we ate many of the chicks, but the writer remembers that Henry Watlin, one cold Saturday night, stoked the wood stove heater full so as to "go off a little piece"; and when he returned, the heat had smothered all the chicks in the top tier of cages.
    A later project of broiler growing was more profitable.

- - -

    Most share-croppers moved onto the farm penniless and with children. Dad usually put them "on the book" and found extra work around the farm. Almost all were men "of their word" and very few accounts went unsettled.
    The following is a typical "on the book" account. A small segment reads:

B. Moore	- February	10,	1940	cash to B. Moore	$10.00
" "	- Feb.	20,	"	"	pd light bill	2.93
" "	- Feb.	28,	"	"	garden wire	3.10
" "	- March	15,	"	"	" seed	2.20
" "	- "	20,	"	"	aspirin	.25
" "	- "	22,	"	" trip to doctor Sat. nite	2.00
" "	- "	39,	"	" Bull Durham tobacco	.50
Etc...		Etc...				Etc...

This account "on the book" never became of much consequence and continued for three years. It was "paid in full" twice and then continued.

A special note: The share-cropper system has been roundly condemned by many uninformed writers; but, at least, it was a survival technique that was voluntary and worked.

December 15, 1940 - Federal Land Bank Loan Balance owed $972.00 to be paid in ten equal payments, due each December 1 at $97.20. Paid the following: Insurance on loan $246.29. Paid interest $216.34. Paid on prior principal $363.01 (The writer doesn't understand it either.)

Hog mineral mix for twenty shoats. 1 gal. wood ash, 1 gal. lime, 1 gal. salt, 1 qt. sulfur -Add a little at a time.
- - Clemons said he worked 5 days last week, 4 days this week - total 10 days @ 35¢ per hr. - $3.50 per day - Owe him $35.00. Advance on book $10.00 - $5.00, owe $20.00.

Cotton Crop 1940

November 15, 1940 sold 9 bales 4146# lint @ 9.35¢= 387.65

November 20, 1940 sold 25 bales 12,390# lint @ 9.1¢=
1,137.69
Total $1,525.14
Less Grinning & Picking   184.66
Gross $1,340.48

Cotton was the cash crop; but remember, most farmers also sold grain, timber, hogs, cattle, hay, and their labor. They also took advantage of their best ability - the ability to do without.

- - -

August, 1942 - Sold peaches - H. Thompson 6 bu. $6.00, W. Page 3 bu. $3.00, N. Page 5 bu. $5.00, etc. for a total of 23 bu. - $23.00

- - -

September, 1942 - F. McWilliams Cotton Crop

Bale no. 694 wt. 493# @ 8.9¢ $42.48
" no. 342 " 500# @ 9.2¢ 46.00
" no. 512 " 500# @ 7.9¢ 33.34
Total monies 121.82
Less pooling   4.20
117.62
Less rent 29.41
Gross $88.21

A hail storm destroyed most of the crop that year. F. McWilliams never farmed again. The "pooling" charge was a marketing charge - farmers collectively bargained for price concession through it.

(Remember that many costs were levied against the gross profit.)

- - -

A 1948 cotton account for C. Jackson who had a gross income of $1,068.96 after he paid his half share rent. Crop arrangements varied because of the input of each party. For example, some share-croppers owned their mules. Others depended upon the land owner to furnish them. The writer never saw - or heard of - a written contract. As far as I know, it was strictly a "hand shake" man "of his word" deal.

- - -

Baled hay in 1949 for public:

                         E. M. Yarbrough 103 bales   16.30
                            Bud Johnson 700 bales 105.00
                        Bridge Rutland 321 bales   48.15
                       Clarence Moody 600 bales   90.00
                                Etc...   Etc...   Etc...

Dad bought a New Holland automatic baler after he sold his dairy herd and did custom baling well into his sixties. He baled in 1949 - 11,050 bales that gross him $1,657.88. (Note that, in general, amounts paid and received are now in thousands instead of the hundreds of the early forties.)

- - -

Sold corn in 1950

          Oct. 26 - To Alabama Flour Mills - 118 bu. $165.87
          Oct. 28 - To Alabama Flour Mills - 120 bu. 160.83
          Nov. 3 - To Alabama Flour Mills - 122 bu. 164.80
Etc...   Etc...   Etc...   Etc...
                    Total $3,534.94

All corn was hauled on a farm truck to Decatur (about 35 miles, round trip 70.) He picked it with a one row New Idea picker into a trailing wagon. From the wagon, the corn was loaded onto the truck with a hand scoop. At Decatur, several hours were often wasted waiting to unload.

A 1951 inventory (done by Dad) revealed a net worth of $65,516,00— with an indebtedness of $6,078. This included 360 acres of the better Tennessee Valley clay soils, several buildings, farm machinery for three tractors, plus the old Goodloe home with twenty rooms.

When the Russian entered the world grain markets, prices improved until the longshoremen refused to load grain at some ports. An entry in 1954 is for grain sold $8,088.00.

Two years later, in 1956 income had improved even more.

Listed sales: Hay - $2,227.10; Grain - $5,401.99;
Baling Hay for public - $12,775.59

Expense for 1956   6,763.89
Net income   5,011.70

(There was no depreciation schedule. It was strictly a "pay in" and "pay out" system of bookkeeping.)

By then, even the longshoremen could understand that wheat was a universal product and if it wasn't loaded at New Orleans it would be loaded at Rio De Janeiro.

Dad often bought steer calves from 300# to 400# wt. in the spring, ran them on pasture grass and sold them the following fall. A steer accounting entry in the early fifties is for steer purchased at 20¢ to 23¢ per pound and sold in the fall at 19¢ to 21¢. This was a profitable enterprise because a steer would double in weight. The usual spread of price in its decrease is much more drastic. For example, in 1991 it was 30¢ to 35¢.

An income tax report for 1959 includes no depreciation

schedule. The writer can only reason that an accountant somewhere kept him from harm's way. A few items listed were: Lights and phone - $147.94 (a full year?), tractor and truck tires - $257.18, cash to bank - $8,212.43 (there is no separation of interest and principal), labor $395.56, living expense $186.52.

- - -

(A notation in the margin of a page) Paid back $9,391.00 borrowed. There is no date, nor other explanation. The rest of the page dated October 15, 1956 is devoted to hours worked by Esau and Lonnie. Listed thus: Esau 5. hrs. Wed. 2.50, Esau 4 hrs. Fri. $2.00. Lonnie 6¼ hrs. Mon. $3.25, etc. etc. (At the bottom of the page) Total labor $198.50.

- - -

An envelope, clipped to page 93, contains a letter and a canceled check. These pages, to a degree, chronicle Aunt Lizzie's struggles after her husband died in the early thirties. Her children had many addresses. One daughter moved to Chicago. Aunt Lizzie's letter is from there, where she had found a position as a live-in companion to an elderly lady. She requests that Dad pay her $500 owed. It is couched in the civility of those times and reads, "If you are able to pay me now, I could use the money." A canceled check for $510 is still in the letter, dated September 18, 1957.

Aunt Lizzie was 99½-years-young when she died. People do not die from hard times - it's the reaction that kills 'em.

- - -

Much business was done by barter. One example was Dad's milk sales to a bottling plant. The plant gave him vouchers to be used for groceries at stores doing business with the bottler. As he used them they reverted back to the plant. This kept the wheels of commerce turning. No one monitored the mark-up at the grocery store. This process became complicated when Dad bartered the groceries to pay his hired help. These accounts are beyond my powers to transfer to these pages.

- - -

This writer enrolled at Florence State Teachers College in the Autumn of 1939 and commuted each day with a half dozen other students from Cherokee. Dad doled dollars (and cents) to me as they were needed for tuition, books, paper, etc. Two years of college were completed this way.

His 'cash' accounts selectively and intermittently show: Dec. 9, 1939 James $5.00 - Dec. 10, 1939 James $1.75 - December 30, 1939 James $4.50 - Jan. 4, 1940 James (Dr. McGraw eyes) $11.59 - Jan. 15, 1940 James (Books) $4.75, etc.

- - -

There are similar entries for my seven brothers and sisters. We all live in relative comfort and by most standards are fortunate. The appreciation we feel is beyond our ability to express.

Ol' Glugly

There is no faith which has never yet been broken except that of a truly faithful dog.
K. Z. Lorenz - <u>King Soloman's Ring</u> 1952

A dog will never forget the crumb thou gavest him, though thou throw a hundred stones at his head.
Sa'Di - <u>Guilistan</u> 1258

HE WAS THERE in the backyard walking 'round and 'round. At first glance, it seemed that he might be playing a game, as though he had reverted back to his puppyhood. And then, I saw the blood on his head and a flowing drip of blood from his good eye. I ran out the back door for a better look. Ol' Glugly's good eye was smashed. He was blind. Blood oozed from his nostril and frothed with his breathing. His left leg dangled, obviously broken.

We did what we had to do -

- - -

It had begun when my Uncle Ralph had phoned me four years before. "There is a pup next door that needs a home in the country," he had pleaded. "It's white with haphazard black spots - looks a little like a Dalmatian, but I'm told it's a cross of bulldog, bird dog, German Shepherd, and, perhaps border collie. I can guarantee that it is also a little bit mongrel."

We had brought the clumsy, big footed puppy home. When we lifted him to the ground from the pickup, he had promptly chased Ol' Tom, our cat, up a tree. In the process, he had crashed into the tree and bloodied his nose.

This was only the beginning.

There were table scraps saved for Ol' Tom, but the puppy seemed hungry. We added a little milk and placed it before him in a dish. The clumsy puppy inhaled the table scraps in "umteenth" seconds, licked the bottom clean, and gnawed at the flowery design at the edges. The plate was rescued and a tin pan substituted. This was filled with dry feed from a sack labeled "Puppy Filler." The dry feed was gulped before we completed pouring; some never reached the pan. We fed him a reasonable meal and then placed the pan under the backyard faucet for water. He lapped several slurps and sat back on his haunches so as to watch the back door from whence the food came.

A pup needs a name.

We had discussed it as we drove home with him. Someone suggested "Ugly" because he was. However, the suggestion was rejected as just a little bit negative. I remembered his gluttony and it came to me in a flash. It was almost as if a light had shone around me. I had heard the word, "Glugly," a combination of glutton and ugly.

And so "Glugly" became his name.

His actions were always direct and unreasoned. When he ate, he ate. When he chased cats, he chased cats. When he fought, he fought. If he adopted you as his master, you were his master.

He adopted me.

I became his master because I was the first to feed him. I fed him often and plentifully. If you opened the back door, he was always there ready to eat. Potato peelings, paper towels (with bacon grease), lettuce leaves, bones, tinfoil were gluttonously gulped. Once I saw him chew a greasecoated light bulb without any obvious harm to his mouth. When he ate, he ate.

But eating didn't do it.

It was not done on purpose: As his lord and master, I was followed everywhere. He ran after the pickup, and one August day he overdid it a bit and looked so bedraggled that I placed him in the pickup bed for a ride home. He learned about *cooolll* pickup riding and the pleasure of facing the wind.

He became a pickup dog from that day on.

But pickup riding was not his downfall. It just helped it along. There were other incidents: one day we leveled an old pond and uncovered several large turtles. It was spring time and soon turtles were waddling all over. Glugly decidedly were mortal enemies and attacked each until all turtle heads withdrew into shells. He then harassed the turtle shells, the protruding tails, and even turned a few on their backs. One large turtle stuck its head out, just enough to provoke an attack. Glugly immediately charged in. The turtle, quick as a trap, clamped to Glugly's nose and held on. The dog, in dog language, begged and pleaded for release; but the turtle was unrelenting. Glugly pulled, screamed, barked, and begged some more. We finally released him be prying the turtle's jaws open.

But he never learned.

A few weeks later we heard him barking down near the creek. It was his "I need help bark." We went down to see and found a large groundhog backed between the tree roots of a tree desperately defending himself. The dog believed that in our presence he might win, so he leaped onto the groundhog and grabbed a mouthful of loose skin and fur. The groundhog squirmed, twisted, and retaliated by sinking sharp teeth into the base of Glugly's ear. Glugly backed away flinging his head about as the groundhog hung on. Glugly flung, shook, flapped, and quivered for several seconds before the pain overcame his fighting instinct. Then he, (and I swear this) he screamed, "I'll turn loose, if you'll turn loose." The groundhog considered the proposition until he thought the lesson was well taught; then he released his bite and ran into his den.

As I said, Glugly never learned.

One day he assumed his cooling position in the pickup

bed as we sped along at fifty-five. A dog barked at the side of the road. Glugly barked back. The dog barked belligerently and Glugly leaped from the truck to do battle — at fifty-five. From the rear view mirror, he resembled a large snow ball rolling down the highway. When we drove back to him, he lay gasping with eyes closed. We brought him to his corner of the garage and gently placed him on his pad. The next morning his appetite was as good as ever. A few days later he had seemingly fully recovered.

I repeat, Glugly never learned or reasoned.

Take the case of rabbit running: he would follow the tractor all day long because an occasional rat, mouse, or rabbit would be disturbed which gave him the opportunity for a chase. Rabbits sometimes darted and dodged back under the tractor. This inevitably happened and Glugly's right back leg was smashed by a tractor wheel. A month was required for recovery.

But more disaster awaited.

One day Glugly visited a neighbor to check out a bird dog bitch and remained past meal time. When his appetite signaled 'eat' he had dashed across the highway to the parallel railway and ran broadside into a passing train. A neighbor alerted me and we brought him back to his corner of the garage. Ribs were broken and one eye had been punctured. A week's rest and plenty of food found him on his feet again. His recovery was gradual and complete except for the eye.

We never knew what caused his last disaster.

Glugly's four years with us were a demonstration of devotion. He followed me and accepted all the food I fed him. He was my friend. Out of the thirty or perhaps forty dogs we've had on the farm I can remember few names or descriptions. I remember Glugly well.

The sound of the gun shot still echoes.

Ol' Blackie and Ol' Blue

Milk more than any other single food furnishes the nutrients for adequate nourishment and good health by people of all ages
                          Encyclopedia Americana

OL' BLUE, LATER renamed "Damned Fool," stampeded in the midst of the afternoon milking and ran through the barn door, without opening it, releasing and stampeding the whole herd.

The first cow I 'really' remember was Ol' Blackie, Grandma's cow, a family pet. Each morning at daybreak, and before breakfast, she milked Ol' Blackie. The milk was really fresh at breakfast.

Grandma felt the need to instruct a six-year-old in the realities of farm life. So, during the year I lived with her, she would call me from a warm bed, and we would trudge to the well to draw water and continue to the barn.

At the barn, she would yell a loud, "SSSSOOOKBOSSYY, SSSSOOOOKKBLACKIE SSSSOOOOKBLLAAACCKYY," into the morning air. Blackie would answer an echoing,

"MMMOOO, MMMOOO." In the meanwhile, I filled a basket with nubbins from the corn crib, added a measured gallon of cottonseed with a discarded lard bucket and sprinkled a little salt from a sack. The basket was passed to Grandma who dumped Blackie's feed into a trough nailed to the crib wall.

Blackie would announce her arrival with a short, "Mmoooo," answered by her calf in a nearby pen with, "BBBAAA, BBAABAAA." Blackie's head would appear as she came around the end of the barn and then walked swiftly, with a salivating mouth, to the feed. Grandma would reassure her because of my presence with a quiet, "Sssaaaaaa Bbllaacckkie," and Blackie would chomp away at the nubbins.

Grandma wet one end of an old flour sack rag and gently washed Blackie's teats and udder as they became distended with milk. The other end of the sack was used to dry them. An old wooden box seat was pushed to Blackie's right side; then, Grandma dashed the remaining water to the ground, set the milk pail under the teats and sat down to milk.

The jets of milk resounded as they hit the empty tin container. "BBBRREAEAEA, BBBRREAEAEA, BBBRRREAEAE," was heard as each hand alternately squeezed streams of milk. Then gradually, as more milk accumulated, the sound changed from soprano - to tenor - to bass. "BBRREAAA, BBRRAAA, BBRRA, BBRR, BRR." This gradually subsided until there was only a "RRR<RRR<RRR." Foam would form on top and create a sound barrier, until finally there was only a quiet, "sssss, sssss, sss."

Ol' Blackie was permitted to nurse her calf at each 'freshening', but the calf was penned each night to insure a plentiful morning milking. When the milk container held Grandma's required volume, we would release the calf for a day of frolic in the pasture with Blackie.

The family cows were gentled until most were pliable as lambs. The calf learned from its mother's example and also became a pet. Any milk cow that didn't gentle would be banished to the herd on the open range and another cow selected.

Another necessary trait was large teats. Otherwise, a

two or three finger inefficient grip made milking difficult. The Europeans had selectively bred cows for large teats for centuries. This resulted in 'overkill' with teats so large that young calves, on occasion, could not nurse. Nursing training was then necessary to start them. The best method was done by holding the calf's head between the herdsman's knees and squirting milk into its mouth. As its appetite was stimulated it would become voracious from the milk taste. A large teat could then be compressed into the sucking mouth. One lesson was usually enough. Sometimes, calves on the range have starved because of the inability to nurse large teats.

But, back to Ol' Blackie: each afternoon, an hour or so before sundown, Blackie and the calf were again brought to the barn. The calf, often hidden in a sunny depression, had to be found and reunited with Blackie, and kept moving to prevent nursing. However, the calf soon learned to nurse Blackie's two back teats on the move. I learned how to prevent this by holding to Blackie's tail, thus displacing the calf.

Grandma would be ready for the afternoon milking when we arrived extra dry to get more cream. After milking I would release the calf I had been holding and remain until the calf finished the teat left for it. Then, I fastened it in the pen for the night.

Ol' Blackie and I became fast friends and developed an understanding. I stopped toting a stick as I drove her to milking and soon she would answer to my call and sometimes come to the barn unescorted. Grandpa was with me one afternoon, as I drove Blackie, and set me on her back. She responded by ignoring me.

Grandpa drove us (the calf, Ol' Blackie, and me) to the barn. She was a good Ol' cow.

Cows are a part of my family history. The association goes back for generations. It must be in our genes. By my eighth birthday, I was a proficient member of the milking crew and I should add, also the barn "cleaner-upper."

My muscles moved silage, hay, manure, milk cans, feed

sacks, manure, brooms, shovels, manure, milk buckets, forks, and manure. On occasion, I also moved dung.

But, I never learned! After five years of being away from the farm, in college and the army, I bought a herd and started my own dairy. That's when we acquired Ol' Blue who was later renamed, "Damn Fool." She was as different from Ol' Blackie as cream is different from hydrofluoric acid.

She had arrived with a group of cows purchased from a "reputable" dealer in Ohio. The war's impact had created a chronic milk shortage and good cows were hard to find. We finally purchased, here and there, about fifty cows, and as they dropped calves, we began milking. After a month we were organized, with milking machines, bulk cooling tanks, pipes, pumps, and automatic feeders.

The cows, crew, and I adapted to the old routine. All the cows were assigned numbers and names, as we noted their idiosyncrasies. Blue's name, of course, came from her color and she seemed to be a good average dairy cow.

Until:

Blue stampeded during the middle of the afternoon milking. Clyde, my helper, said, "She sniffed the air, then she bellowed and ran through the barn door without it being open." No self-respecting cow ever skips a stampede. So, the whole herd followed her out of the barn through the smashed door. Clyde's wife had just walked by and she said it was the most frightening thing she'd ever seen.

Clyde and I repaired the door, rounded up the cows, (after they calmed down) and finished the milking without Blue, who was renamed "Damned Fool" by Clyde.

We were forewarned and after that day left Damn Fool in the catch lot until the other cows were milked. We'd then bring her into the milking parlor last - just in case she might stampede again.

And she did: she was being milked last, in the parlor, when she bellowed a warning, kicked the milkers off, climbed over the retaining bars, and bolted into "the wild blue yonder." Sarah had just walked up to remind me of a movie date we had planned. She said, "Damn Fool created the wildest sight I have ever seen."

Two stampedes had occurred just as women walked into the dairy area! Could it be that Damn Fool's fits were caused by women? Was it their cologne? The sight of them? Their hairdo? Or 'sumpin'?

The next day we corralled Ol' Damn Fool and asked Clyde's wife to walk by. Sure enough, Damn Fool tried to climb the planks of the corral fence. She ran into the gate. She bellowed. She pawed the ground. It was pure madness!

We loaded her into an enclosed truck for sale at the stockyard and felt relief as she was driven off. Women come to the saleyard as spectators. I wish I had seen what they saw.

This rambling tale is to remind me of the uniqueness of all the hundreds of cows I have known. Perhaps, even to remind me THAT I LOVE ICE CREAM IN SPITE OF OL' DAMN FOOL.

Ol' Glugly and the Coyote Bitch

It was 3:00 a.m. on a warm spring night with the red gold moon setting in the west. Ol' Glugly, my devoted dog, and I were the only living beings in the three hundred acre field we were plowing. The scent of honey suckles mingled with the diesel exhaust from the six cylinder motor of the Moline 1350, as it roared at full throttled power, while pulling the six, eighteen inch bottom breaker through the red clay soil. We (Glugly and me) had been plowing since we had relieved Clyde at midnight. The four floodlights, mounted above the cab, created a giant bubble of illumination. From my vantage, I occasionally caught glimpses of a shadowy dog-like animal near the edge of the field. Ol' Glugly must have scented the animal, because he stopped, in mid trot, directly before the tractor with his ears laid back, and he pointed like a bird dog in the shadowy animals' direction.

- - -

One deluge after another had kept us from the muddy fields that spring as cotton plantin' time arrived. The rains had finally ended and we began full time around the clock plowing. Clyde and I never rested the Moline except for servicing.

Ol' Glugly had faithfully followed me the full two days. This entailed eight hour shifts behind the tractor, back and forth. He did miles of plodding.

This tirelessness wasn't altogether motivated by devotion. Remember, his name, "Glugly" was a combination of 'glutton' and 'ugly.' Mice, rats, rabbits and even moles were disturbed as the red clay was turned. Glugly made the most of a bountiful opportunity. Sometimes, he would catch a large rabbit and miss several rounds as he ate it. As I said, Ol' Glugly was devoted to his provider.

He had missed only four breakfast feedings in his two years on the farm. Those drastic departures from his normal behavior had happened about two months before this story began. Bits of rabbit fur littered the backyard. So, I assumed that he was hunting rabbits and had dulled his "breakfast" signal and appetite with rabbit meat.

Ol' Glugly stopped, in mid trot, directly before the tractor. His ears laid back and he pointed like a bird dog in the shadowy animals' direction. An instant later he launched himself like a heat seeking missile, in a straight run toward the animal. His body language hinted that his run would end in a confrontation of blood, gore and mayhem.

I shifted the Moline up to "fast" as I raised the plow from the red clay. The circle of light was enough to keep Glugly in sight, and as I approached, I saw that the animal was a coyote. An encounter ending in slaughter or, perhaps a headlong chase seemed inevitable. Either would be interesting.

But, nothing happened!

Ol' Glugly bore in at a dead run, and the coyote never moved! Instead it groveled in abject subjugation and obeisance, with its tail sweeping against the ground, in complete canine submission. Ol' Glugly recognized the rules of canine nature and came to a dead stop. Then he walked stiff legged around the coyote. Their common D.N.A. heritage has not changed very much during the eons that separate them from their common ancestry.

Mice, rats, and rabbits had also attracted the coyote and the dog should have obeyed his territorial instinct. He naturally should protect his food supply and rout the coyote. However, nothing happened?!

    Light from the tractor continued to bathe the scene as I throttled back in curiosity. The coyote was obviously nervous, and reluctant to stop its instinctive ritual. Ol' Glugly must have sensed the need to break off the encounter because he ambled toward the trees and brush. The coyote followed in long running bounds, disappearing into the brush and dark with him.

    But not before I had seen that the coyote was a female, with teats that had been recently suckled. The bitch coyote had a young litter of pups somewhere nearby.

    Ol' Glugly had missed four breakfast feedings over two months ago.

    Do you suppose----?

left to right -
James McWilliams, Evelyn McWilliams-Jones, Helen McWilliams-Neff, Jack McWilliams, C-1926

"Motorcycle Gang"
far left - Andy McWilliams, *second from left* - William C. McWilliams, *center* - Grandfather McWilliams (with ankles crossed) C-1916

left -
W. C. McWilliams and Cora Cook McWilliams - "Mamaw"

above, W. C. McWilliams in front of the old Fairview Farm House - site of the present TVA Garage. *C-1905*

below, W. A. McWilliams on a Mogul International Tractor on land then owned by the McWilliams' family. Now known as Spring Park in Tuscumbia. *C-1912*

Memories

To be able to enjoy ones past life is to live twice.
    Martial - EPIGRAMS A.D. 86

ON IMPULSE, I TURNED OFF the paved road onto the dirt trail leading into the woods, and leading back a half century in time. The old trail was once a busy road, but now it was almost impassable, with weeds, small trees, and deep ruts left by the last deer hunter's pickup. My eyes peered ahead as I crept down the hill and finally saw it still standing there.
   White paint had flaked away from the sagging weather boards, leaving the old church a dirty grey color. Many panes were missing from the windows as wasps, dirt daubers and other insects buzzed in and out. The old steps were eroded and cracked. Gravel crunched under my shoes as I trudged up and into the building. Inside there were dust, spider webs, old song books, Sunday school literature, an old cardboard fan, an abandoned shoe, a fallen bird's nest, and the bare floor. The old hand-made benches were gone. Water stains on the ceiling and the rattle of loose roofing confirmed that there would be more decay. It was just another old abandoned building wasting away in the decay of time.

But, oh, the memories:

It had been the religious and social center of a rural Appalachian community for decades before the brick church had been built out on the newly paved road. Family, kinfolk and friends had always attended, twice on Sunday and occasionally on Wednesday. There was a revival every summer after the crop "lay by" time, and "an all day singing and dinner on the ground" in late summer.

The singing and dinner day was extra special and attracted former friends "back home." There were those that "never darkened the doors" who came to enjoy egg custard, or, perhaps, apple cinnamon sugar coated pie, and fried chicken, on that special day.

I retraced steps back outside and found it so quiet that I could almost hear my memories. A woodpecker sounded a, "Rat atatatatatat," near the top of the old oak with the low limbs, where the mules and horses had been tethered, while still hitched to wagons or buggies. (The Model T's and other motorized vehicles were parked separately because horse drawn wagons steered erratically). The old hitching oak stood at a distance of perhaps fifty yards from the church. The distance helped mute the smell of mule dung.

A half century and more had flown by, but my nose still wrinkled in remembrance. Caught up in nostalgia, a song came faintly to my ear and built to clarity: My memory heard it clearly, "When the roll is called up yonder - when the roll is called up yyyooonndder - when the rolll is cccallled uupp yyyooonder - *whenn thee roolll isss cccallledd uupp yyooonder I'll beee thererer."*

As my memory returned, Grandma's clear soprano voice pealed out high, loud, and free, above the other female voices while she swayed to the rhythm of the song. At five feet five inches, she stood in middle-aged stoutness wearing her usual homemade, grey, gingham dress that billowed about her and swept to the floor. Iron grey, curly hair framed her assertive face with its high, beak-like nose. Blue eyes sparkled behind spectacles, she referred to as "specs," that had been purchased at the General Store, from a tray, for two dollars. A large, long-toothed comb held a big bun of hair at the back of her head. A few loose wisps of this moved with each stroke of a palmetto fan swinging to the rhythm of the song, while beads of perspiration dampened her brow and upper lip.

In my reverie, my memory saw her clearly. She looked exactly as she did on that other day long ago.

The "all day singing and dinner on the grounds" was the social high of the year. It rated higher than Christmas. New clothing was worn, if you had it. Boys and girls of courting age primped, powdered, perfumed, combed, curled and fantasized.

Grown-ups also reacted: Housewives wanted to maintain their reputation as cooks. Song leaders practiced their voices and tuning devices. The local carpenter checked the old picnic tables and children had to prove an ability to consume more food than ever. (There were no finicky eaters in those days.)

Grandma's reputation for fried chicken had to be maintained. It was a matter of supreme importance to her. So on that day - that Sunday "of singing and dinner on the grounds" - we began her fried chicken project early. She summoned me and we walked to the woodpile as she shelled corn. At the woodpile she trilled a, "Here chicachicachick - here chicachicachick" while scattering grains of corn at her feet. Chickens soon flocked about her while she inspected them carefully and snatched a young rooster by its leg. Then she instructed, "Hand me that ax and hold this rooster's head over the chopping block." One "whack" and I held a rooster's head with no chicken attached. The chicken was placed in a convenient basket, where he flapped about, spattering blood only in its confines. "Throw the heads in the basket, too," Grandma commanded. We did four more fryers and then toted the basket, (me on one side, Grandma on the other) to the nearby wash-pot and dumped the chickens into it.

"Roll up your sleeves," she directed as she hurried to the kitchen and soon returned with a kettle of boiling water and a sharp knife. The water was poured over the chickens and sloshed about to assure thorough wetting. "Just one minute of scalding," she reminded us, "We don't want to set the feathers."

"They've scalded enough. Now take them out by their feet and lay them across the bench and start pulling feathers off them. Hurry up! Move!"

Surprisingly, the feathers came off easily. It was no big deal. As I handed each shorn chicken carcass to Grandma, she did a final plucking and singed it with a flaming corn shuck. She then gutted it with the knife, being careful to save the liver, gizzard, craw, and heart. A pan of cold salt water received each part as she skillfully dismembered the carcasses.

Within twenty minutes, I had plucked a tub of feathers for future featherbeds and Grandma had processed five chickens into a dish pan of cool salty water.

Two large frying pans simmered away on the old range stove less than an hour after we had walked to the woodpile. A warm delicious smell of fried chicken guaranteed Grandma's fried chicken reputation for another year.

A picnic basket of assorted pies, breads, jams, and other goodies was prepared and covered with a table cloth. Fried chicken was carefully packed into a second basket, with a hot brick to keep it crispy, and then we were off to the "all day singing and dinner on the grounds." Baskets were placed in the care of the ladies dinner delegation when we arrived and we entered the church where singing was already in progress.

And that's when they sang the song that remains in my memory, "When The Roll Is Called Up Yonder." A six year old country kid is often confused: We had removed chicken feathers with a "scald" of water. The word was firmly programmed into my memory. I knew what it meant. I did not know what a "roll" was, nor did I know "up yonder."

The words, "When the roll is called up yonder" sounded more like, "When the roll is <u>scald</u> up yonder" to me.

Grandma thought it hilarious when I tugged at her sleeve and asked, "Grandma, how do they scald a roll?"

- - -

I returned from my memories when a loud cawing came from a crow clowning in the woods, back of the old dilapidated church, "Caw-Caw-Caw-Caww."

The crow is a wise old bird. I laughed too.

The Floatin' Gang

No race can prosper till it learns that there is as much dignity in tilling a field as in writing a poem.
                              Booker T. Washington

As I scanned the obituaries, the name "Jack Howley," instantly caught my eye. My memory saw him as the youngest member of the "floatin' gang;" a cheerful towheaded little barefoot boy of nine, who couldn't keep up with the gang and was always assigned a row between two grown-ups who helped him through the worst grass and weed infestation.

At the funeral parlor, his face was recognizable as Jack's face, but the wrinkled brow, weathered face and grey hair framing it, reflected the sixty years that had flown by since our days as members of the floatin' gang. Days that were less complicated; days that, in our nostalgia, seemed happier.

Jack's older brother was there. He had also been a member of the gang from long ago. The ties of friendship were as vital and alive as though we had sweated in the cotton fields only yesterday. Our faces mirrored the emotions and memories we felt, memories of yesteryear and the floatin' gang.

Before the development of herbicides and other exotic chemicals, it was necessary to rid cotton rows of weeds, grass and surplus cotton plants by manual use of the hoe. As a result, many rural and small town kids of the South became proficient cotton choppers.

A farmer's success at cotton growing depended upon the number of hoe hands he could field. This was especially true when there was excessive rain to prevent the mule drawn cultivators from plowing ahead of the hoeing.

An average family, of six to eight members and a team of mules, could handle forty acres of cotton if weather permitted. When cotton germinated to a stand, most farmers cultivated continuously to reduce the manual hoe work. But mule and manpower had its limits. Saturday and Sunday were rest days. This was a necessity.

Work hours were from sun-to-sun or, as it was explained, "from can-to-can't." There was no effective lighting for night work so farmers attempted to use all daylight hours. A late planted crop was unproductive and a "lost" crop, from weeds and grass could not be tolerated. Economics and pride were strong incentives for long hours of work.

But nothing remains the same. Soon, the tractor's horsepower made mule power secondary and eventually obsolete. One man with a tractor could farm a hundred acres or more. With head lights and endurance, one man could drive almost continuously. However, during the first few years of tractor powered agriculture (the transition period) the techniques for cleaning the cotton rows of weeds were not developed. Manual hoeing was necessary. It was still possible to lose a crop when rains prevented access to the fields.

- - -

Dad thought it was going to be the very best of times in the late 1920s. In his optimism, he purchased a Farmall Tractor and all the attachments. Then he persuaded four share cropping families to double their usual acreage by promising to help with the tractor, if they fell behind in field work.

With help from the tractor, the cotton was planted on time and came up to a good stand. Then it rained. The weeds and grass also germinated, and it rained. The weeds and grass grew, and it rained. The grass, weeds, and cotton grew more, and it rained. The grass, weeds, and cotton became verdant, and it rained. The weeds, grass, and cotton resembled a hay crop, and it rained.

Farmers sat around Boss Keeton's store front, sipped five cent Cokes and swapped hard-time tales. One old-timer told about the year when no crops were gathered and people survived the winter by hunting, eating turnip greens and "doing without." A young farmer listened and "allowed-as-how" he was considering abandonment of his crop and moving up North to Detroit for work in the Ford plant with his brother.

And then finally, it stopped raining. After a few days, the upland fields dried enough to cultivate. Then, all the one row mule drawn cultivators and the Farmall tractors set to work. However, the hoeing lagged because individual families could not coordinate hoeing and cultivation with the uneven drying of the upland and lowland. Hoeing was spasmodic as the situation grew from discouraging to desperate.

That's when Dad had his brainstorm. He imagined that, if all the families agreed, they could combine all the hoeing crews into one large hoeing gang and thereby, become more efficient - a task force for cotton chopping. Plowing would proceed ahead of this force during the day and the tractor, with lights, would do the follow-up cultivation at night.

The families all agreed to his plan. One housewife accepted the work force's book-keeping chores. Two water boys were selected to lug water to the crew. A wagon was equipped with a water barrel, a grindstone, extra hoes, a canvas covering and one Grandma volunteered to baby sit. Sam and Bess, our oldest mules, would pull the wagon as hoeing progressed.

All able bodies people reported to the field the next morning. Hoes were sharp; dinners (noon meal) were brought in gallon lard buckets; the water barrel was filled and drinking cups were available; Grandma came to babysit three little ones; all preparations were complete for a full day of hoeing. There were thirty people ready for hoe duty - sixty rows to a round!

Grandpa had noted the preparations with interest. Soon after we began hoeing he joined us with his special garden hoe in hand. "I'll walk along and help the young-uns keep up," he had explained. But, by mid-morning the sun's heat forced him to seek the shade. But not before he had observed our rapid progress. "This gang moves from end-to-end and from field to field just like it was floatin'. I ain't never seen nothing like it. You should call yourselfs the floatin' gang," he observed as he walked away. So we became "the floatin' gang."

The gang was an ordinary gathering of people; ages were from the babies to Grandma, who was seventy. A few individuals had graduated from the local high school, but would have seemed only semi-literate by today's standards. One lady, Mrs. Jackson, had once sung with a quartet and would sometime render a haunting ballad. Her <u>Frankie and Johnnie</u> and <u>I'll Take You Home Again</u> were sung in such an enthralling manner that all chatter ceased and we found ourselves hoeing to the rhythm of her song. It would be a gold record, if sung and recorded today.

There was the usual small talk between we kids but observant parents took care to separate the "talkers." The head of each family was the "boss" in his crop and closely checked our work. Slow choppers were assigned rows between faster workers. Mothers hoed near their playful children. All was arranged with efficiency in mind.

On a typical day, hoeing began early in the cool of the morning. Dew and dirt soon muddied our feet and ankles and also stuck to hoes. The hoes could be cleaned by striking a rock or another hoe. This kept a constant bell-like ringing in the air. There was the superstitious belief that if you accidentally hit another's hoe, you would hoe together again the next crop year.

The faster choppers would alternately help the slower ones, and, at the ends, as each finished his row, they in turn helped another until all were finished and ready for a breather.

Straw hats were worn by all except a few older women, who wore bonnets. Overalls and shirts were worn by the boys and men. Girls and younger women dressed in slacks or brother's pants. The older women retained their loose gingham dresses. Most clothing was faded and patched. It would be a fashion statement in today's denim market.

There were no restrooms in the fields. Nature's call was answered by a discreet visit to the nearest thicket. The boys and men would go to the left, the girls and women in the opposite direction. Older people sometimes went home to check the mail box or to fetch a forgotten item.

Love struck teenagers would pair off on adjacent rows but alert parents upset such romantic maneuvers by assigning the girl a row near her mother. We boys also noted this aberrant behavior and badgered our friend unmercifully for being sweet on Mary - or Jane - or any girl.

Laziness and laggardness were not tolerated. We did the hoeing right. Johnson grass, with its long roots, had to be dug up and left in the middle to be plowed at the next cultivation to prevent rerooting. Crabgrass received the same treatment. Cotton plants were thinned to the width of an eight inch hoe, two or three plants per clump. As I said, laziness and laggardness were not tolerated.

"The floatin' gang" continued for a few seasons until new chemicals and techniques made it obsolete. When farming responded to the Industrial Revolution, things changed. New families, new members, new conditions brought changes. But the spirit, the goodwill, the fellowship, the camaraderie of people with hoe in hand infused our lives with its purposeful example.

I know now that "the floatin' gang" provided good training for all people. This was especially true of the young.

The older brother and I stood remembering a cheerful, little tow-headed barefoot boy of nine. The brother observed, "It's been such a short time."

Orilla's Secret

OL' CHESS, our twenty-year-old horse, lunged up the bank of the creek and almost dumped the sack of salt from the saddle horn. Dad had released his hold on the sack when he reached behind the saddle to prevent me from sliding off Ol' Chess's back. We had ridden three miles back into Orilla's hollow to bring necessary salt to the "free range" herd and to count the cows and calves. In my six-year-old imagining it was as adventuresome as riding the Santa Fe Trail to the big roundup.

The lead cow's unevenly clanging bell could be heard when we stopped and listened. The sound came from across the hollow, about a half mile away. "They're over near Orilla's house," Dad observed, as he guided Ol' Chess to the bell, while crooning a loud, "Sook, Sooookk, Ssooook," in a monotone. The bell quieted. "She's listening," Dad said, and continued his, "soookk, sssooookk, sook." Then we detected a low, "mooo, mmooo, mmmoooo." "That's Ol' One Horn," Dad realized as the bell began a new rhythmic ringing. "They're coming to us."

While the herd hurried across the hollow, Dad tied Ol' Chess's reins to a low limb and dismounted, with the salt sack in hand. He distributed a heavy pouring of salt around the base of two large pine stumps and then dumped the remaining salt on a large flat rock.

Cows and calves came hurrying from among the trees and immediately began hungrily licking and slurping the salt. When we were certain that they were all out of the thickets, Dad counted them twice and discovered an increase of three new calves. All were in good flesh and without any obvious need of attention. The tally was correct, so our task for the afternoon was complete.

A woodsmoke smell hung in the still pine scented air of the hollow with a hint of bread baking, or something akin to it. Dad sniffed the air and said, "It's probably Orilla's tea cakes cooking."

"Who's Orilla? Why does she cook tea cakes way back here in this place?" I had inquired.

Dad explained, "Several years ago, when Orilla was younger, before World War I, she loved and married a man from over the mountain. When the United States entered the war, many men from this area volunteered to go whip the Kaiser. I was one of them, Orilla's husband was another. He was in the trenches for several months and died in a gas attack. Orilla, in her grief, fled back here to this hollow and an old log cabin. She could not be persuaded to return home. Her family made the cabin as comfortable as they could. They also gave her necessary furniture and left two old hounds for protection. She and the hounds remain here to this day. By the way, the original dogs died from old age, but not before two litters of puppies came along. The dogs with her now are puppies she raised. They are extremely loyal to her." Dad continued, "She has a small pension from the army, but it is not enough, so she sells cakes to make extra money. A coupla times each month she walks "out," followed by her hounds, and sells cakes to anyone she meets. There is now a regular customer route that buys all she has to offer. They taste good and, at a penny each, are a bargain. You ate some last week, the cinnamon sugar cakes, remember? Let's ride over to her house and see how she's doing."

Barking, baying, snuffling hounds met us in a melee of confused greetings as we approached the cabin clearing. They circled about Ol' Chess' legs with wagging rumps and whipping tales, signaling "welcome" but demonstrating ownership of the territory.

A woman yelled at the dogs from the front stoop of the old house where she sat stirring a dish pan of yellow dough. Chickens surrounded the stoop, pecking and scratching as though just fed. They ran under the house as we approached and the woman repeated her command, "Shut up you dawgs; shut up and com' 'ere." The dogs quieted and retreated to the woman.

"That's Orilla," Dad said.

She was dressed in old faded, patched blue denim. Her rough dress consisted of a jumper, shirt, overalls and an old flour sack that hung from the bib of her overalls. It was up front for handy hand wiping. She assured us, "Them dawgs won't bite 'less I tell 'em to; get down and set a spell; a batch of cakes is 'bout done." Her sleeves were rolled up to her elbows, with hands and lower arms liberally coated in cake mix.

"I see you got your little boy young-un with you, Bill. He's a likely lookin' one; leave him with us and we'll fatten him on cakes, fried chicken, baked rabbit, eggs and turnip salate." She laughed. Then wistfully added, "My young-un woulda been older'n him if he had'a—," but she broke off and stirred her dough vigorously.

A prominent nose dominated Orilla's good natured, weathered face, with a mass of gray-brown hair over it, bound by an old felt hat held in place with a frayed leather shoe lace. Rough brogans, worn without socks, hung loosely laced from her feet.

Bright blue deep-set eyes, with a lingering sadness, smiled at us from under a furrowed prominent forehead. "Go on. Get down. Them hounds is harmless," she insisted, as she replaced a well chewed, sweet gum, snuff stick into her left cheek.

When Dad dismounted and set me on the stoop's edge,

the dogs protectively surrounded Orilla. "Git offa me, you mangy hounds," she protested, as she slapped the most aggressive one with an open palm that had just stirred dough. The slap left a well defined handprint on the hound's rump, this was instantly licked away by the other dogs. Knowing a good taste, the dogs crowded Orilla even more as she flailed about with the same punishing rewards. Sensing a dog fight building, Orilla scrambled to her feet and retreated to the cabin door. "This dough is mixed enough, anyhow," she explained as the door slammed behind her.

Dad checked his pockets and yelled at the closing door, "Bring us a quarter's worth of cakes. Make them cinnamon sugar if you got 'em."

Orilla reappeared a few minutes later; sure enough, she had a hot pan of cinnamon-sugar cakes, that gave off the most appealing, appetizing aroma ever smelled by a six-year-old hungry country boy. "These oughta hit the spot," she bragged as she counted two dozen and three cakes into, our just emptied, salt sack. Dad placed a quarter and a dime on her palm and received a graceful, "Much obliged." Orilla then inquired about news of the community. They "passed the time of day" about "outside" happenings and we were soon astride Ol' Chess on our way home.

Dad began munching cakes before we were out of the clearing and shed of the escorting hounds. He handed me a cake over his shoulder and I refused it. "Don't you like cinnamon-sugar cakes?" he questioned.

"I like them but I can't forget those hands slapping the dog while mixing dough," I answered as I visualized dogs with dough spattered rumps running about.

"Remember those cakes you ate last week? Those were Orilla's. You enjoyed them then. Those were the same cakes as these, only these cakes are much fresher and still warm," he reasoned. "Those dogs are as clean as your hands were when you stuffed your tummy last week. Besides, the heat from baking kills the germs in the dough. Think about it! Orilla's cakes are tasty. There's an old folk saying, "Everyone will eat a peck of dirt in his lifetime." Forget Orilla's cooking habits and enjoy these delicious cinnamon-sugar cakes. Also, let's keep Orilla's cooking habits a secret. OK?" he advised.

"OK," I answered, "You and I can keep any secret." Both my hands appeared in front of him, as I hugged from behind and demanded, "Give me two sugar-cinnamons." Dad gave Ol' Chess free rein, as we reflectively rode toward the creek.

Smoke from Orilla's baking hung low in the still air reminding me of her haunting words: "My young'un would a been older'n him if he had a—"

The Treasure Trove

OUR PLANS were to remove the roof of the old mansion after we had salvaged the interior. That way, rain, sun, wind, and falling debris wouldn't mar the valuable "stuff" we wanted to reuse in the new home we were to build. We removed the doors, door frames, mantlepieces, light fixtures, heart pine flooring, and other ornate or intricate pieces. Chimneys were then dismantled, brick-by-brick and the brick cleaned and stacked. The stairwells were next in our plans.

I had begun loosening the plaster from the underside of the old service circular stairwell when a metallic sound alerted me. Something different fell into the clumps and dust of fallen plaster. I searched and discovered and old half blackened silver coin. In the dim light I could read, "United States of America" - 50¢. The reverse, when cleaned, revealed "1831."

- - -

The old home had been listed, "For Sale," by a local real estate agency for more than a year, but remained unsold. The listing continued as Dad became more and more discouraged.

Finally, on a clear April day, he confessed to me that he wanted to rid himself of debt and some responsibility. He explained, "The old home is too big for Mamaw and me to rattle around in at our age." He proposed to trade me the old home and land for a small farm we had recently acquired. This would consolidate our land holdings and the extra equity Dad would gain could be used to build a smaller more comfortable home free of indebtedness.

The "deal" was done and we became the owners of a large old southern plantation home which we soon discovered to be a "white-elephant."

As a farm family just starting out, the old mansion was beyond our dreams of renovation into a comfortable family home. The heating cost alone was astronomical. Paint, plaster, hardware, labor and all other costs were beyond our means. Times had changed!

A year was wasted as we wavered between attempts to sell it and revival of dreams of renovation. Our problems was solved by a friend with building experience, when he suggested that we dismantle the old home piece-by-piece, store the material in nearby barns and rebuild a home that met our needs from the salvaged lumber, bricks, etc.

That is what we did.

A description of the old home may be of interest to the reader: The old Goodloe home stood on a hill overlooking Mulberry Creek and its small valley. Several old cedar and oak trees surrounded it, permitting only a limited view through the foliage. Four tall Ionic Greek type columns stood in pairs at the center of the home supporting a large dormer with a matching half circular window. A square stone pedestal in front of each pair of columns was occupied by an imposing Mastiff St. Bernard type cast iron dog who guarded the entrance in regal quietness.

Behind the columns, a veranda was partially recessed into the front hallway. From it, a large oaken door, with elongated window casements, opened into the hallway that extended through the home to the rear where a replica of the front door admitted onto the full back porch.

From the second floor, a smaller veranda or balcony rested in a quiet extension above the front entrance. Admittance was through a smaller version of the front door. A cast iron balustrade surrounded it emphasizing its cool coziness behind and near the crown of the columns. It was the most calming breezy nook known to man on a hot summer night. A dry moat, twelve feet wide and ten feet deep, extended before the home and half way along each side. Ornamental iron railing guarded it from atop retaining walls of large hewn mortared limestone. This large moat was designed to admit light and air into the basement which served as a social and gaming center. A wine closet and bar occupied a central position. The front veranda served as a bridge over the moat and also as a shady roof over the doorway that led into the moat from the basement.

The entrance hallway, with fifteen-foot high ceilings, was centered with a small chandelier hanging by three chains from an oval molding that artistically displayed cherubim, fleur-de-lis, buds, leaves, and other figures. To the left, a wide stairwell clung to the wall as it rose in a gentle curve to the right and entered the second floor hallway. Banisters of heart cherry wood continued beyond the stairs in a continuing circle that enclosed an opening from the lower floor into the upper hall. An airy open well was thus created that permitted a cool flow of air and also enhanced a sense of spaciousness.

A stair, directly beneath the main stairwell, led into the basement with its two large rooms and wine closet. Each room had a fireplace and three large windows with built in benches. Steps led up from these rooms to identical roofed patios on opposite ends of the home. These covered patios joined the back porch creating a large sheltered area across the back and along each side to the moat railing.

A pair of small porches at opposite sides allowed entrance through two smaller hallways from these entrances to the main hallway, thereby giving access from all four sides of the home. There were many ways to enter or leave. (Imagine the parties in 1856.)

Eight stairwells of varying size and style interconnected the two floors, half floor and basement. One circular stairwell mounted through an unlighted area and in our childish imagination harbored "buggers" of all varieties. Games of chase or hide-and-seek could be played to perfection. Sliding down the long main staircase bannister was really "something else."

There were two fireplaces in the basement; four on the first floor; five on the second floor and one on the top floor for a total of twelve. Even if there had been chain saws to speed the work, it would have been a fire-wood providers night-mare.

Convex panes protruded from the windows. These created a reflected glare that distorted any view of the inside from the outside while the view from inside, though also distorted, was fairly clear. One way glass is not new.

An old dog-trot log cabin had been incorporated into the rear of the old mansion. It supposedly dated from the early 1800 s and was built by Indians before the Trail-of-Tears. The old log walls were covered inside with plaster and outside with heart pine weather boarding. Thick, well insulated walls resulted. Flooring was heart pine, an inch thick and smoothed with some type of planing device.

Framing, for the newer addition, was heavy heart pine beams, assembled with the mortise and hickory peg method, much as the Amish build barns today. No nails, spikes, or bolts were used. All openings, other than doors and windows, in the framing were filled with brick and mortar. Heart pine weatherboards were then applied over the brick. The inside walls were plastered and then overlaid with stark white plaster-of-paris. These three layered walls were the best insulated walls in their day.

Ornate plaster moldings joined walls and ceilings. Wainscoting and shoemold contrasted the stark white walls with the lower woodwork. Eye catching oval or round plaster-of-paris moldings-rosettes-medallions decorated the ceilings of the main rooms and hallway. These ornate features imparted a palace-like look, while the stark white walls and ceilings inspired a cooling sensation even on the hottest days.

There were thirteen large rooms, four hallways (or two if you count the cross halls as part of the main hall), a half dozen miscellaneous closets, two large attics and two roofed patios plus the full back porch.

A mechanical system of wires and levered hinges connected to spring mounted bells, was installed to summon servants. As a boy, I remember only the bells with dangling wire high on the walls in disrepair.

Two large cisterns provided soft water through guttering, pipes, filters, and hand pumps. The clear soft water was superior to the lime saturated water from local wells. I might add that there was no awareness of the danger of lead poison because all gutters were assembled with generous amounts of lead soldering.

A separate kitchen smoke-house combination of solid brick, except ceiling and roof, was built close by the home. It was attached by a covered walkway. The old swinging pot rack in the fireplace was the only evidence of the buildings past history when we dismantled it.

No hint of any toilet facilities were in the old home. It is probable that chamber pots and water pitcher-bowls were the only accommodations. Dad installed two bathrooms in 1926.

It is rumored that it was spared from burning during the Civil War because, the owner, Mr. Calvin Goodloe was a congressman with influence in the Federal Army. After the war, he moved to New Orleans in the service of the Federal government and sold his Alabama holdings.

There was little upkeep to the home before we moved into it in 1926. Afterwards there was a constant maintenance struggle.

When we (Sarah and I) acquired it we soon recognized that repair and renovation were beyond our means. That was our reason for dismantling it.

Our salvaging had continued for sometime when I heard the metallic clink and found the old coin.

- - -

I reached into the hole from where the coin had fallen, and discovered more coins and papers. Excitement, almost like fear ran through me. My thoughts raced wildly. The paper could be old bank notes. Perhaps they were thousand dollar bank notes! Maybe the coins were gold! I was rich!!

An old bucket sat nearby. I held it under the opening with my left hand and nervously swept coins, paper, and debris into it with my right hand. "Clunkety clunk clunk clink clink," it sounded as I carefully brushed everything into the bucket.

After methodically exploring the cracks and crevices of my treasure trove, I took the bucket outside into the sunlight to gloat over my riches.

The paper was only bits of an old paper sack that likely had held the coins. There were no bank notes. The coins were not gold, but fifty old half-dollars and two quarters, for a total of $25.50. But, they all had dates before 1861, with two from the 1700s. I assure the reader that I did not use them in slot machines or for the purchase of R.C. Colas and Moon Pies.

SLICED LIGHT BREAD

Go thy way, eat thy bread with joy
                                                    Ecclesiastes 9:7

THE NEW TOTALITY SHOPPING CENTER EXTENDED in a blaze of fluorescent glare as far as the signs, symbols, emblems and trademarks permitted the eye to see. The hum of unlimited consumption could be heard from all directions. We purposefully wheeled our shopping cart from aisle to aisle in search of the many selections on our shopping list. It was a shopper's wonderland. Food, clothing and shelter (a large tent) could be purchased. All necessities were available under one roof. A branch bank was there to replenish funds. A pharmacy was available for medication. Food beyond belief was everywhere and the mind's sustenance was guaranteed by books, cassettes and other educational material. All customer needs were foreseen and satisfied. "A happy customer is a consuming customer" was the center's secret motto.

We came to the aisle labeled "Cereal, Bread, Crackers, Tacos, Cakes, Cookies, Saltines, Wafers, Etc." The bread section alone had more than half a hundred selections. Rye, wheat, corn, oats, buckwheat, canola, rice, and many exotic mixtures were on display. Colors ranged from dark brown pumpernickel to pale white rice bread. Cracked grains, sesame seed, and various condiments were added for more appeal. There were long loaves, round ones, fat square shapes, bread sticks, and even loaves that were baked into shapeless chunks for the connoisseur. A saleslady with a microwave distributed small slices of the bread-of-the-day, with cheeses or spreads. The smell of fresh-baked bread wafted its pleasant fragrance around us.

It was a miracle recognized by only a few, because this bountiful display could not have existed when I was a child. The variety was pleasing, but it was the slicing that intrigued me for a short time ago all loaves were sold as baked. And here was thin sliced, table sliced, toasting sliced, canape' sliced and even half sliced! Biscuit doughs, packaged in layers, separated when cooked. Even some small loaves were sliced lengthwise for submarine sandwiches.

I stood in a trance remembering.

It was a cold day with intermittent wind, snow and sleet in January of 1930. The black unheated Model T Ford school buses with canvas shuttered windows had all been late because of the muddy roads, or else because of the inability to get them cranked on time. The pervading pernicious malaise of the cold had slowed everyone. We students had warmed by the pot-bellied wood stove after our cold bus ride. Then Miss Maud had summoned us to our desks just as a messenger walked over from the high school to inform us that school would turn out an hour early so that buses could finish routes before roads became impassable.

A flu epidemic had spread colds, coughs, and runny noses to all school personnel. There was a constant interruption as coughing caused by the hot air spread through the room. Snotty noses required occasional relief and a few needed to visit the outdoor toilet after our long, cold bus ride from the far reaches of the county.

It was a Thursday, four days since our Saturday night bath. Most had remained unwashed because of the cold and total lack of modern plumbing. Also, families ate a limited diet, with beans dominating the menu. Our stomachs were a gaseous cauldron that regularly reacted. The heat also generated vapors from our clothing as we warmed. We stunk - as in skunk - in the unventilated room.

Later, Miss Maud glanced at the swirling snow and instructed Angus McQuade to "Throw more wood in the stove and open the damper a little more." We were doing long division of ten problems written on the blackboard. It was almost lunch time and our study period was up. We country kids were looking forward to an escape from the room into the cold and freedom so as to eat our lunches in the lee of the schoolhouse, away from the stench.

As the papers were passed, Miss Maud walked to the windows and thoughtfully watched the wind, sleet and snow. The bell rang and she signaled, "Quiet," with her left hand held high. And then she did it! She declared, "It's too cold and windy to eat outside today. I suggest that you remain at your desks. Afterwards, you may go to the toilet, but with your coughs and colds, remain inside as much as possible."

Miss Maud's suggestions were her commands. We squirmed in our seats. The implication was overwhelming. Our brown paper sacked lunches were to be blatantly unwrapped from its newspaper coverings for everyone to see. Soggy grease soaked biscuits with hard fried sausage or cold runny fried eggs were to be displayed. Some biscuits held only half-fried fat back. Those with lunch buckets might open small fruit jars of yesterday's beans, stew, buttermilk or other farm kitchen fare, supplemented only with cold corn pone. We were about to be exposed before the class as "pore folk."

You see, we customarily ate our lunches in semi-privacy under the trees, in the doorways and even under the eaves, if there was only a little rain. Sometimes, the press of play was so strong that we ate "on the run" as we played One-Eyed-Cat, or Mule-and-Driver, or perhaps Chase-and-Base. No matter where we ate, we could maintain a certain privacy as we unwrapped our lunches. Pride was of the utmost importance and a "pore man's lunch" should be eaten in privacy.

The consolidated rural schools of the early 1930s had no lunchrooms. Students either brought lunches or fasted the ten to twelve hours at school and on the buses. This long day was a strong incentive to bring a lunch to school.

In contrast, some students lived in or near the small cross-roads towns where the schools were built. They had access to the general store and, also were often children of more affluent homes. Their lunches were usually sandwiches of "light bread" purchased at the store and spread with peanut butter, potted meat or sliced cheese. Sometimes, even the crust was trimmed. These students boldly unwrapped sandwiches for all to see. They then fastidiously ate with curled finger sophistication. A few, it was whispered, even had sandwiches containing green lettuce (cow feed!). The banker's son often brought prepackaged cakes and a bottle of Coke that went "sssssttttt" when opened with a special tool kept in his pocket.

And we were expected to eat at our desks!?!

If only we had had "light bread" we could have faked our otherwise poor lunch and eaten with impunity. With "light bread" one could even spoon beans and neatly nibble the crust from the edges of "light bread" without shame. "Light bread" signified an escape to a wider world, to a new sophistication.

But on that day of cold, coughs, and stench, we ate inside and remember it even now. A few escaped humiliation by eating in the corner back of the stove. Those at desks unwrapped biscuits under the desk's hood. This writer remembers, however, that he left his lunch uneaten until the long bus ride home.

An added note: "Light bread" at five cents per loaf was a bargain - if you had the five cents. Thin slicing could make a loaf last and last. "Slicing thin" was an art and became an obsession with certain pupils who ate on the steps near the

Principal's office. The contents of these ultra-thin sandwiches were revealed at a glance and, in derision, loutish students claimed that writing could be read through them.

The Totality Shopping Center featured a loss leader of four loaves for a dollar. They also displayed one loaf for two dollars. The boast on this loaf was "No Fat! No Cholesterol! Almost No Calories! Great Taste!"

We live in an amazing time. There was no corn pone.

G. T. T.
(GONE TO TEXAS)

SINCE COLUMBUS SAILED WEST in 1492, the attraction of the West has motivated more and more people to follow his example. We seem inspired or motivated to follow the sun. It makes for a longer day or something.

And Texas, to the West, especially has lured the people of Alabama, Tennessee, Mississippi, and Georgia. Most families of the Southeast have kinfolk, friends or acquaintances there. This has been true for almost two centuries and probably is the reason Texas is a state in the United States of America and not a Mexican state.

It isn't so much that Southerners wanted to go to Texas, it's the fact that Texas had open space to the West. This impulse to "move west" was intensified by the Civil War and other subsequent events and even today cousins, acquaintances and friends move to Dallas, Houston, Livingston, Ranger, and other Texas towns.

But before and after the Civil War there was a constant traffic to Texas. It was the place to go when one needed change, space or sanctuary. It was the place of a new start when troubles came and one needed an escape. This escape was used so often in the Southeast, that the term "G.T.T." became common language understood by most everyone.

- - -

If Teresa McCorkle hadn't been so cute, with her red hair, blue eyes and freckles, the trouble wouldn't have happened. Just turned eighteen, she was fully a woman with curves that couldn't be concealed with the full skirted dresses so fashionable in 1904. The wasp waist configuration of woman's clothing was especially attractive on her, and enhanced her good looks from the waist up, especially her face.

Added to this was an impetuous flirtatious nature that attracted all males that saw her. Angus McQuade came near and was attracted. His attraction became an infatuation that became a passion, a burning desire almost beyond control.

Angus' father had given him a young black gelding horse, named Jet, for his twenty-first birthday. The animal under Angus' care became the most magnificent horse in the community. He routinely curried Jet and also, when weather permitted, rode him to the creek and bathed him. The horse and Angus became inseparable and were a pleasure to see as they attended the all-day-singing-and-dinner-on-the-ground, parties, and other events of the community. Jet and Angus traveled as far as twenty miles from home. (Jet was the equivalent of a red convertible in today's scheme of things.)

Angus's mother had died at his birth and his father had concentrated his devotion on Angus. It was a responsible devotion that had resulted in Angus' early maturity. At twenty-one, he was a man of responsibility. He was also handsome, with a strong square Irish face and ruddy complexion topped with dark reddish hair. His compact body of one-hundred-eighty pounds looked taller than the five-feet ten inches he stood. Physical activity from his rural life made him walk as gracefully as an Indian in him prime.

However, he did not practice patience, fortitude, or peacefulness. Angus could and would fight anyone that gave him a reason. He was implacable when he fought and many predicted this would be his undoing.

Teresa McCorkle saw him before he saw her at the Crooked Oak singin' and dinner. She was with her latest beau, Linus Carrolton, who was sporting his Dad's new rubber-tired buggy and the Arabian stallion. Angus was "taken by surprise by Teresa's rovin' eyes" when he and Jet cantered up to the hitching rail.

As soon as dinner was "on the ground", Angus found a mutual friend and was introduced to Teresa. An animated conversation began that excluded her date, Linus, and before the food was eaten, Angus, with Linus listening, persuaded Teresa to let him visit her home the following Saturday afternoon.

Come Saturday, Angus finished his chores, saddled Jet and was on his way to the McCorkle home in neatly dressed splendor topped off with a generous splash of bay rum. His heart sang in anticipation and Jet, glad to be free of the pasture's enclosures, had to be held in check to prevent him galloping full out.

But Linus Carrolton and two friends had made other plans. At a bend in the road, where tree branches created a dark shade, they stretched a rope across it at a man's height while riding a horse. The rope caught Angus under his chin and dumped him into the dust of the road. The impact to the cartilage of his larynx was the most painful hurt Angus had ever known. He lay writhing in pain with dust choking his mouth, eyes and nose. When he had recovered enough to stand he found Jet waiting expectantly nearby. Angus slowly and painfully remounted and rode him back home.

Upon arriving at home, his father insisted that he go for Dr. Riley, who came and examined the raw rope burns; he swabbed them with iodine and wondered in amazement that Angus was alive. He advised no talk and a few days' rest until recovery was assured.

Angus wrote Teresa a note of explanation that was

delivered by a friend the next day. Later, another date was arranged and Jet and Angus were successful in their journey to Teresa's home.

Angus's adversary for Teresa's favors, Linus Carrolton continued to see her at every opportunity. Sometimes, when Angus was absent, Linus thought he might be winning Teresa's favor because she, in her impetuous ways, found it difficult to ignore any male attention.

But before the summer was over, it became obvious that Angus was Teresa's favorite. Linus developed a smoldering hatred that burst into flame when he saw Angus and Teresa kissing in semi-darkness one hot August night.

The next morning Jet was not at the barn when Angus walked down to feed him. A search in the pasture found him at the far corner with a bullet hole in his right eye and an exit wound near the top of his head.

Angus was more than devastated. A deep, dark, deadly hatred consumed him. There was only one reason for his living, and that was as an instrument of death for Jet's murderer.

He left Jet where he had died, and walked purposefully to the farm shop where he honed the large blade of his pocket knife to razor sharpness. He then went to find Linus.

Linus had just emerged from the rear of his father's mule barn when he saw Angus approaching with knife in hand. Angus flatly stated, "You ought not a'killed him."

Linus, fully aware of his predicament, and the knife in Angus's hand, became agitated and reason abandoned him. "I ain't killed him", he answered "and I didn't hire Hank Shoddy to shoot him either. I ain't had nothin' to do with no shootin'. And it was Hank that stretched that rope 'cross the road, too. I ain't done nothin'," he concluded.

"No one knows about the rope except my father and Dr. Riley except, of course, the ones that stretched it. And no one knows about Jet being shot except me and those that done it," Angus said, and then continued, "Even if you didn't shoot Jet, I know now that you're responsible and I'm gonna kill you for it."

Linus turned to escape but Angus tripped him; then fell upon him and began a butchering process he had learned well at the hog killing each winter. It ended only when two sharecroppers from the barn came running out and wrestled him away from Linus. They held him long enough for Linus to escape with blood running over his shoes.

"He's gonna bleed to death," one man observed.

"You go on home now," the other advised. " 'Cause you done done 'nuff harm to him."

Angus walked home and washed his hands. He then found his father, explained what had happened and concluded, "I hope he bleeds to death."

By mid-morning word had spread throughout the community. Many of the Carrolton kinsmen gathered at the home place where Linus was being sewn together by Dr. Riley, who confided, "If he lives it'll be a miracle."

A Carrolton cousin allowed as how "I'm ready to go on a lynching party. Go get your guns if you ain't got 'em, and meet me at the crossroad in half an hour. We'll hang Angus McQuade to that oak at the bluff."

The lynching party met as planned and a dozen men rode to the McQuade home. When there, they demanded that Angus come out or they would "come in and get him."

Davis McQuade, Angus's father, stepped onto his elevated front porch with his old ten gauge shotgun. Both hammers were cocked as he held it to his shoulder. "I wish this hadn't happened," he began, "but Linus asked for the cuttin' by what he done. Now y'all go on back home 'cause I ain't givin' up Angus. If y'all try to take him, two or more of y'all are gonna get killed and y'all will probably get me. That's three dead'uns up 'till then and Angus is standin' by the winda with my ol' forty four and he knows how to shoot. Now y'all go on home."

The Carrolton's considered for a minute and the cousin allowed that, "We'll go talk it over but if Linus dies, we'll be back."

Angus left his home that afternoon dressed as a working woman in the company of two other regular workers at the

McQuade farm. There was a sack over his shoulder with a change of clothing, a hundred dollars in his wallet, and the address of an aunt in Texas. The Memphis Special ran at six p.m., with Angus on it, still dressed as a woman. "G.T.T."
Linus didn't die, but was a cripple for life.

Four years later Angus returned from Texas. In his absence, most people agreed that he had had reason to "cut" Linus. He never returned to Texas, but remained in Alabama the rest of his life and the Carroltons never threatened him again.

Teresa, in the meantime, married a well-to-do banker, had two children and, when her husband established a branch bank in Dallas, she too was G.T.T.

Home From The War

You can't go home again.
                                    Thomas Wolfe

 THE WAR had crunched on, consuming men and machine year after year. I had been away from home for three Christmases. Many others had been away much longer. Memories of home had faded, except when there was a letter or we heard a song.
 And then, there were rumors that the war was winding down.
 Most soldiers learn to discount rumors, so there was little reaction when we heard that the Germans had surrendered. Later, when General Eisenhower made the official confirmation, the reaction was still muted. We felt more numb than elated. Men sat or stood about in small groups and talked quietly. Others stood or strolled alone as if in deep thought.
 The years of excitement and boredom, of hurrying and waiting, of cold and heat, of hunger and feast, of noise and quiet, of terror and calm, and of death and life had created an emotional numbness, a wasteland of non-reaction. As the day progressed, those on duty continued the routine.

Those off duty retired to their tents for letter writing, reading or rest.

Thoughts of home remained unspoken.

One of our more perceptive sergeants collected soap, cigarettes, candy, and such and requisitioned a jeep. He drove into a nearby French hamlet and returned with several bottles of wine. The happy hour began. By late afternoon, realization and conversation were in full flow. Home! Family! America! There was the real possibility that we would be goin' home.

That night, a pilot pilfered a crate of signal flares, flew over the French countryside, and created a fireworks display. In an attempt to outdo this celebration, a drunken soldier sat fire to an abandoned Luftwaffe bomb and ammo dump. The resulting explosion blew him to bits. The concussion and shrapnel was felt and seen for miles around. No one else was injured, but our euphoria came to an end. Home was still far away.

Our air base, near Paris, became an evacuation center for P.O.W.s and refugees. We were operational weeks after the surrender.

Russians were flown to Moscow and certain death, and P.O.W.s to England and a return to life. Food and other necessities were delivered whenever the need arose. We saw VIPs and the lowly pass through on their way home. Home was still far away.

Then one day we were instructed to dismantle and move to the French coast near LeHavre. Rumors were that we would relocate in China for the invasion of Japan. The French seaports were grid-locked with military traffic; we waited weeks before boarding a ship. The ship's crew revealed that our destination was New York. Home was not quite so far away.

The long passage was spent mostly below deck, so crowded and packed that alternate breathing was suggested. The cold of the North Atlantic could be felt, on the below water line, of the steel hull. The medium sized troop ship rolled with the waves like a waterlogged barn door.

There was seasickness, and pig sty conditions soon existed. We complained less and less because home was not so far away.

Early one night, the engines stopped! Motion ceased! Word came down the passageways, claiming that we were anchored off Coney Island. That Ferris wheels were turning and lights were bright! A city without blackout! Home!

One by one, we stole on deck. It was true! There were lights all over! We were drawn to the railing as if by a magnet. Hundreds crowded to the landward side of the ship. We were mesmerized by the sight. Our hypnosis was broken by a red flare and an urgent voice ordering us back to quarters. We had almost capsized the ship within sight of home.

Back in quarters, one man was sobbing uncontrollably. Inquiry revealed that he was from Brooklyn and had seen the street light in front of the home that sheltered his wife and three-year-old daughter he had never seen. His home would be in sight with the sunrise.

Docking was accomplished next morning and dozens of genuine, vocal, pretty American girls, were there as an unofficial greeting committee. (Thank you God.) Camp Kilmer welcomed us with clean clothing, clean water, clean bedding, clean barbershops, and delicious food. Travel orders were expedited and I was on a train to Atlanta the next day. A vendor provided a bacon, lettuce, tomato, and mayonnaise sandwich in Richmond, where a friendly girl sat opposite me and inquired, "Hy theah soldjuh, wheah yuh goin?" Home was so very close.

Three days in Atlanta and I was given a three week furlough. There was an interval between buses in Birmingham and I bought a civilian suit, shirt, tie, and wing toed shoes. The Trailways bus stopped at every crossroad, but we finally came over the mountain and saw the lights of the Tennessee Valley at 2:00 a.m. The lights of home!

My Dad came for me in his old Dodge pickup. His face was contorted by his effort to smile through his emotions. We shook hands as two true-blue old soldiers and drove home.

The folks at home were also war-weary. They had coped with shortages, rationing, worn-out machinery, and waiting. My mother was as I remembered. My five sisters and two brothers, seemingly, were more than just three years older. They were now teenagers and adults. Home had changed.

A boyhood friend had died early in the Philippines from a sniper's bullet. When I encountered his father, we shook hands briefly; then he walked slowly home.

An elderly acquaintance met me on the street of the county seat and said, "Hi, Jimmie. I haven't seen you roun' lately. Where you been? Must have been stayin' home."

My attempts to contact old friends from school days was frustrating. Most of them had also gone to the war. Others were married or had moved away. They had also left home.

The Pacific War ended abruptly with the destruction of Hiroshima and Nagasaki. I returned to Atlanta and was mustered out of the Air Force. When I returned to Alabama, the realization gradually came to me. The time and place of my youth was long gone. Home had changed.

Technology has accelerated change to an undreamed of degree. This rapid change has alienated much of mankind from his origin, his beginning - from his home. Thomas Wolfe says it best. "You can't go back home to the someone who can help you, save you, ease the burden, back home to the old forms and systems of things that once seemed everlasting, but which are changing all the time - back home to the escapes of Time and Memory."

Nostalgia, the poignancy of memory haunts us all to some degree. While we cherish our humanity, perhaps we should refocus and see our home as through the eyes of the cosmic travelers.

A Message to Miss Miller

IT WENT "SPLAT" as it hit Miss Miller, our first grade teacher, under her left ear where the jaw and neck join. The chalk ceased its dry scratchy sound as she turned from the blackboard with a surprised unbelieving expression. A fat juicy paper wad was stuck beneath her left ear. It gradually slid down her neck just as her thumb and forefinger squashed it. She brought the gooey mess of pulp before her eyes and shuddered when she realized what it was. Her revulsion was more than human sensitivity could stand. She collapsed into her seat as waves of nausea overwhelmed her and only then did she belatedly fling the gooey mess of spit and paper into the waste basket.

It was Pride Tate's fault. The new toys he was always inventing to show off at school started it. For example, he had whittled a string spun wooden top with steel spinner point from an old farm wagon wheel spoke. And then, he had made a rubber band powered spool tractor that would run a full three minutes because of his special invention, a P & G soap washer/regulator. But his slingshots, called flips, were a special creation. They shot V-shaped pieces of wire with bullet-like velocity. Another model would launch seasoned ragweed stalks like an arrow for great distances.

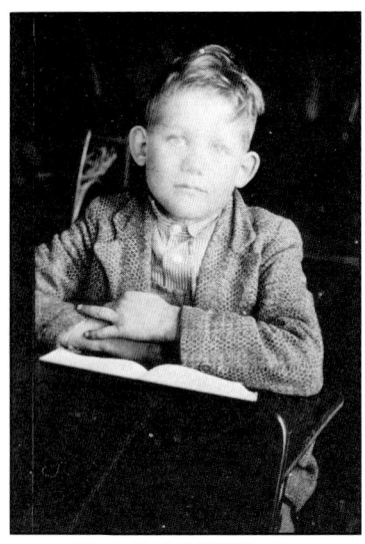

Jimmie McWilliams

Once he built a wagon with wheels sawed from a twelve-inch diameter hickory log. An inch thick and shod with straps of tin for tires, the wheels, when installed on his home built wagon, let him ride like royalty each noon lunch period with a team of boys hitched by means of a discarded plow line rope.

But it was his pebble catapult that caused the trouble. Simple in design and made from material available to all, every school boy had to have one.

Pride's catapult or "shooter" was easy to make. It was a thin board one inch wide, one-quarter inch thick and ten inches long; at first sight it resembled a ruler. Made from seasoned springy hickory, one could shoot a great distance by grasping the lower end in the right hand and aiming as you pulled the top back with the left while holding a pebble in place. Upon release you could almost hear the "whish" and "zing zing" from its imagined velocity and ricochet.

Of course, Pride's shooter was an elegant version with a friction tape-wrapped handle and an indention to hold its projectile securely before a shot. It was the very best.

I had to have one.

Our farm shop had a miscellaneous collection of old wood from the many repair jobs done there. My search soon located an old banana shipping box with foreign words on it. The boards were the right size and well-seasoned. Springy beyond belief, they could be bent into a C-shape before breaking. With pocket knife, saw, and wood chisel, I fabricated a shooter two inches longer than Pride's.

When tested with pebbles, peas, peach pits and other

projectiles it shot with precision. Even spit paper wads did well when propelled from it.

(Reader, don't anticipate; I'm doing the writing.)

Pride Tate set me up. He toted the shooter in his belt at his left side for an easy cross body draw with the right hand. Securely held upside-down in his belt, the shooter when drawn was ready for instant shooting. With the left hand one could place a pebble while simultaneously bending the shooter back. Tate could draw and shoot in one second flat.

Until the beginning of this story there had been no problem. And, there would never have been one if we had not had the target shoot-out during our lunch period. My shooter, made from exotic South American wood two inches longer than Pride's, had consistently outshot everyone's - even Pride's.

After lunch and the shoot-out, I had swaggered in self-exaltation to my desk with my trusty shooter stuck in my belt, ready for any adventure. Miss Miller was writing our homework at the black-board and instructed us to copy it in our tablet. The task was boring and when she turned to her desk for an eraser, I lapsed into day-dreaming. The chalk and board made a dry scratching sound that lulled me further into a reverie. I became lost in a dream world of adventure with my trusty shooter at my side.

    As I crept through the enemy lines with the message I was to deliver to the lost battalion, I was captured. Quick as a flash, the message written on a half sheet of tablet paper was jammed into my mouth for chewing and swallowing. My captors attempted to pry my lips apart to prevent this. What should I do?!?

    Quick as a flash, I drew my trusty shooter and shot the chewed and dampened message beyond the enemy lines to the lost battalion. It was done in a half second; twice as fast as Pride Tate's best shot. The enemy cursed in defeat and wrote my fate on a black-board.

Black-board!!!

There I sat in awful realization as Miss Miller turned and unstuck the sticky wadded message from her neck. A white handkerchief was snatched from her desk as she collapsed into her chair, sick with revulsion. As she wiped her neck dry until it was red, the gooey gob remained in her left hand. With awakening realization she flung the message into the wastebasket and shivered in continued nausea as she attempted to cleanse her left hand.

- - -

After recovering from her nausea she stood before us in suppressed anger and demanded, "Who shot that paper wad?" No one answered. "All right," she continued, "I'll go down each row and question you one by one."
She did as threatened and came to me. "Did you shoot it?"
"No, Ma'am," I lied with a bare face. (Hence the term 'Bare-faced lie'.) It was my first conscious, serious attempt at a deliberate falsehood and I did pretty well, if I say so myself. The event is as clear in my memory as the beginning of this paragraph.

On Miss Miller's third circuit, she threatened to keep the class in the room during all subsequent lunch periods until the guilty student confessed. With that kind of pressure being applied, I confessed, was paddled and had my shooter that was made from exotic South American banana wood confiscated.

To this day I can't figure out how I so precisely and accurately delivered that message to Miss Miller.

The Town's Clown

HIS MOTHER ADMITTED that he clowned as a baby. There had been no yowling crying fits when his diaper needed changing, or when he was hungry. Instead, Smiley Jones gurgled, smiled and cooed to get adult attention. And, both parents admitted that Smiley received more attention and care than his brothers and sisters.

Once, when he was just two, he had followed his father across the backyard in a pantomime of long swaggering strides. On another occasion his mother watched him as he mimicked his big sister applying make-up. He was not only a natural comedian, but also a sensitive, instinctive observer of human nature even as a child.

Smiley's ebullient, intelligent disposition attracted a wide range of friends as he grew older. Boyhood companions flocked to the Jones' home at all hours. In school, teachers noted his ready smile, compliant nature and ease of learning. They probably gave him higher marks than he deserved. In kindergarten, little girls gravitated to his sandtable because of the many innovations he brought to sand castles. Later, when there were church or school socials, he was at the center of the activities.

Things came so easy for him, especially the art of making

people smile. This infectious good nature projected so positively that many responded with smiles before they knew him. The urge, the impulse, the inclination could not be resisted; he was a natural clown.

Once, he observed to a local merchant that his 'sale' prices were higher than his 'everyday' prices. Another time, in school, a math teacher had posted the wrong answer to a long problem. Only Smiley, of thirty students, disagreed and diplomatically persuaded the teacher to agree. This unusual observation and other things he was reported to have done or said were remembered and most people could identify the Jones' boy, Smiley.

Smiley was average in his physical appearance. At eighteen, if desired he could pass unnoticed in any American town. His hair was brownish-blond depending on the light. His nose was neither upturned nor straight - just average. His build was neither stout nor slender. He was whatever one's eyes wanted to emphasize. His appearance offended no one.

But his amiable cordiality, his attitude of undeserved friendliness instantly impressed most who met him. Few people found any reason to dislike him. It was inevitable that the more daring, adventurous boys of the town found him to be a willing companion in their search for entertainment and diversion. Smiley became the leader as they did all the small town pranks: Tin cans were tied to the constable's car. The town's tall water tank was spray painted with football scores. Watermelons were pilfered from gardens and farmer's fields. Newspapers were shredded over friends' (especially girls') yards. Someone spiked the punch at the school prom. Potatoes were stuck up the exhaust pipes of buses that brought visiting football teams. Smiley's gang did all the usual small-town capers.

As his life was frittered away, Smiley spent more and more time at his avocation - practical jokes. Also, although he drank little, he spent much time with young men who did, and as a result, their practical jokes became more outlandish, even bizarre.

He and a co-conspirator were expelled after they were seen mixing firecrackers into the school's coal supply. He did not return after his month's probation and quit school in his senior year to devote full time to idleness and practical jokes.

Some of the more memorable are still recounted. For instance, an alcoholic, stuffed-shirt salesman, caught between towns with an insistent thirst, came to Smiley seeking information as to the town's bootlegger. His patronizing manner toward the "local yokels" prompted Smiley to direct him to the town's most ardent prohibitionist preacher. In ten minutes, the salesman was back protesting that he was unsuccessful and had received a lecture on the evils of alcohol.

Smiley, detecting an opportunity for a really professional type practical joke, apologized profusely and explained, "I forgot. Mr. Smith was arrested last year so now he sells only to a special select few people. He's careful. There is a password - actually, a sentence of passwords that may seem a little strange. He's extra careful."

"What is it?"

"The words are, 'Sister Keenly is up in the Kingdom.' Say it twice and a little louder the second time." To clench the joke, he gave the salesman two dollars and requested, "Bring me a pint since you're coming back this way."

The poor salesman had no way of knowing that Mr. Smith was not only an ardent prohibitionist but also the preacher that had conducted Sister Keenly's funeral in a rickety old frame country church a month before.

With the casket before him, Mr. Smith had ardently praised the virtues of Sister Keenly's life, and had finally concluded the funeral rites with the words, "Sister Keenly is up in the Kingdom." With this pronouncement he had brought his heavy arms and hands down to the frail railing between himself and the casket. The hefty shove broke the railing and Mr. Smith fell across Sister Keenly and the casket.

Smiley and the gang fled, after secretly watching the

salesman's confrontation and the resulting chase back to the town square where Constable Hank Clinton had to wrestle Mr. Smith away from the salesman and restrain him as the salesman fled.

Once, when a wrecked auto sat near the railroad crossing where traffic came to a halt, they placed a dressed store front dummy in the car's front seat with a liberal splash of red paint. Then they wedged the dummy's head in a hole in the windshield with a flow of paint beneath it. As alarmed drivers and passengers stopped with rescue in mind, Smiley and his gang, hidden in nearby bushes projected their voices through a large pipe. "Please put my head back on! My ol' body needs it!" Thankfully, the town constable was alerted before any permanent harm was done.

Sometimes, Smiley did the tall-tale act: If strangers were at the local cafe, Smiley would dress in his rich-dude clothing and, with the connivance of the waiter, sit at an adjoining table with a friend. A typical conversation of rich-dude talk would begin: "Did you put the Lear in the big hangar or in the machinery shed?"

"The big hangar, sir."

"The taxidermist is supposed to pick up those rare Tibetan snow leopard skins today. They may start molding if we don't get them out of the forward cabin today. Be sure to phone him so he'll know where they are."

"I called an hour ago."

"By the way, check with the State Department again about our clearance into Patagonia next Tuesday. I can't wait to fish again on Lake Titacaco. Those Andean giant mountain trout are a real fishin' treat."

"The State Department has cleared us and I also spoke with the Andean Minister. His son wants to fly home if we leave tomorrow."

"Tell the son to meet us in Miami when we land to refuel. Also, remember if you want you may bring your girlfriend along because our flight crew is short two people." These charades would continue and, if the stranger responded to his friendliness, Smiley would soar into eloquent grandeur, posturing about his wartime flying with General So-and-so.

Constable Hank Clinton once fell into the group's disfavor and became a targeted victim-to-be. Smiley with his organizational ability developed a plan to lock Hank in his own jail overnight.

Smiley and two co-conspirators spread the word that they were "gonna get fallin' down drunk" and soon afterward appeared on Main Street acting as though they were. Hank, as was his practice, advised them to "go on home 'fore I hafta put you up." Smiley insisted that he was his own man and would go home when he was good and ready. With gestures, staggers and a fallin' down, he convinced Hank that he was really fallin'-down-drunk. Hank half walked and half dragged him to the calaboose and barred the door.

The calaboose was a reinforced wooden building with a sheet iron covered door fastened from the outside with two stout hickory two-by-fours. These were hinged at one end and fitted into a slot at the other end.

Hank's policy for the unheated jail was to hold drunks until they were sober and then release them. Smiley shivered in the jail and shortened his drunk act by an hour. Hank was summoned by a passerby that Smiley knew and he was immediately released.

Smiley emerged pretending sickness and bent over as though he were vomiting. Feigning weakness, he asked Hank to get his coat from inside the jail. "I feel so bad," he begged.

Hank fell for the plea and entered the jail. Smiley slammed the door, barred it, then drove Hank's car to City Hall, where he wrote a note and placed it on the dash reading, "Gone home for the night."

Shouting from the jail effected Hank's rescue at daybreak. Smiley left town for a month's visit at an aunt's home in Memphis.

Some episodes were downright mean.

Spring Creek ran just beyond the edge of town. Flowing with crystal clear water from two large springs, it was and had been for generations, the favorite swimming hole. However, the owner rented the land to a new tenant, Mr. Rex Lommax, who placed a "No Trespassing" sign near the creek and chased swimmers away several times. Later he threatened them with a shotgun and actually shot into the air causing several boys to abandon their clothing and other possessions.

The "Divine Right" of boys to swim on hot August afternoons in Spring Creek was challenged. Smiley and gang quietly arranged to rebalance the scales of justice.

They began with a two gallon bucket of fresh hog manure that outstunk any skunk. This was mixed with the offal from a twenty pound catfish. This malevolent, malignant, miasmic, malodorous mixture was left to simmer in the hot sun for two days.

Then the third night at midnight the mixture was ladled into a reinforced grocer bag, which was rolled into grease soaked wrapping paper with several fire crackers for good measure. This "contraption" was carefully placed on Mr. Lommax's concrete front porch and lit as the doorbell button was fastened down. The gang retreated to a nearby thicket and observed as Mr. Lommax flung his front door open and attempted to stamp out the flames while firecrackers went off and the awful mixture flowed over his porch. His house slippers and silk pajamas were ruined because the scent of hog manure stinks forever - and forever. Unthinkingly, he went back into his living room over the carpet and sat on the new sofa.

The next day a warrant was issued for persons unknown.

On another occasion the town's miserly bachelor, Mr. T.E. Titeman became interested in buying a thrifty car. The Volkswagen was recommended and after two months of dickering he bought one and persuaded Smiley to teach him to drive. With a month's instruction he became able to putt-putt around town and began bragging about his gas mileage.

Smiley had heard a radio show about a similar situation and the practical joke that resulted. He saw a golden opportunity: With the filling station attendant's help, he began adding extra gasoline and soon Mr. Titeman bragged that he was getting seventy, eighty and even almost a hundred miles per gallon.

Smiley then reversed the process at the filling station by pumping less gas than was indicated. Mr. Titeman began complaining, drove the car back to the dealer and threatened to begin walking once more.

The dealer advised him about what was probably going on. Mr. Titeman threatened to sue the station owner, but finally gave up because of lack of evidence. Smiley was never directly implicated. The local citizens still tell about the gasoline caper and laugh at each telling as though hearing it for the first time.

- - -

Smiley lived at home until well into his thirties, at which time he met Maudie Bassham who was as fun loving and devious as Smiley. Within the year, she had married him and moved him into a new home. A friend helped him obtain a job at the local factory where he moved rapidly up to a position of significance. More advancements were possible if he had had a high school diploma.

Inquiry revealed that tests were available that could bestow a high school equivalency diploma. Smiley took the test and amazed the proctor by passing with the highest score ever achieved.

The proctor, intrigued by Smiley's accomplishment suggested that he take a standard I.Q. test. This was done and Smiley's score was near the upper limit. The score surprised everyone, especially Smiley.

"With your mind you can do or be anything you wish," the proctor had explained. Smiley exactly understood the implication of the score and its effect on his life.

"No one will ever top this one," he ironically reflected.

"Tar" Peterson

KATE, A FEMALE DONKEY (OR JENNY) and Tar were friends. But Kate, even in her servitude, asserted her donkey independence by often pacing ahead of her owner, Tar. As their day continued, Kate's natural exuberance was worn down from toting the two containers of melted resin and Tar might be out front; or again, when the road permitted, Tar would walk with one hand on the containers to dampen the way of Kate's load. They seemed to be mutual toilers rather than donkey and master.

Tar and his jenny made an unusual sight as they trudged the rural backroads of the area. The writer remembers the small gray big-eared donkey with a container on each side of her pack saddle as they slowly appeared up the hill before our home. Tar poked along beside Kate in overalls and jumper with a sweat-stained floppy gray felt hat firmly set on his head over a turban-like head cloth. His attire had accumulated tar spots and grime from several days of peddling. A week's growth of facial hair emphasized the good humor from his eyes and the hidden but obvious smile. When he spoke one forgot the beard and clothing and instead recognized a man of some distinction.

No one could tell when Kate and Tar might appear with

pine-resin-tar to sell. Sometime they might stop by every six months and then not return for a year. Probably they peddled their ware when they had a surplus or needed funds. Also, it was rumored that Tar was sick and in his infirmity made fewer "runs" from his pine resin cooker.

The cooker was built with the simplicity of necessity. It reflected a common-sense approach to life: Four green pine timber ports were set into the ground on the lower side of a three foot high embankment. These posts, in a five by five foot square configuration, were the same height as the embankment. A platform of heavy two-inch thick timber covered them and, in turn, were sheathed on top with metal roofing. A fireproof coat of red clay mud dried into an adobe brick-like finish, served as insulation for the platform. A small two-inch opening was left in the center for the drain pipe of the cooker that sat atop the platform.

The cookpot was the essential component. It was the usual type cast iron pot that most farms found indispensable in those times. Its many functions included water heating with an open fire for laundry, bathing, scalding hogs (for hair removal), floor scrubbing, etc. Ashes were also leached in them to obtain lye, and later lye soap could be made in them. Tar's converted thirty gallon pot had a piped opening in the bottom and a snug fitting lid; otherwise, it was not different.

His raw material was rich pine wood, often called "pitch pine", which he scrounged from the surrounding forests and lugged to the cooker on his back, until he later acquired Kate and a two-wheeled cart. Old pine knots, roots, and heart wood, all pine resin impregnated, were piled above the cooker. When enough was gathered, Tar sawed, hacked and split it into small fragments until he had a potfull. The lid was then secured and a slow smoldering fire was started around the pot. This heated the chips until the resin melted and drained from the bottom pipe to a collecting pan. It was then ladled into storage cans.

This "natural" pine tar from aged rich resin wood was judged superior to ordinary tar purchased from the general store. The ordinary tar was the by-product of the turpentine industry and came from "green" un-aged pine sap. Tar's tar was different and found a ready market.

Tar had arrived from the Memphis train on a Monday morning in July. The station agent had politely spoken to him as was his custom and Tar had introduced himself as John Peterson and inquired about available work. A bystander, overhearing the conversation, had referred him to a stave mill (barrel staves) six miles back in the hills. At the mill he had been hired on as an off-bearer for slabs.

He was a steady worker and "took hold" easily and within a month became the head sawyer. At the end of the season and at winter's onset, the mill owner hired him full-time to care for the cattle and other farm related work. This position entailed a cattle roundup with the usual de-horning, dipping, castration, and branding. Tar (the product) was liberally applied as an antiseptic, cauterizing agent, insecticide, and coagulant to stop bleeding. Halfway through the last day of roundup, the tar bucket fell from its perch and spilled. Operation came to a halt as the owner prepared to travel the twelve mile roundtrip for more tar. John Peterson volunteered that he could easily make more tar from resin wood. Under his direction resin wood was gathered and a make-shift old tub cooker with a hole at one side was soon dripping melted resin into the tar bucket.

Because of his resin-tar knowledge, John Peterson became known as "Tar" Peterson, and in friendship fellow workers shortened it to "Tar."

His accent and his speech patterns indicated more than an ordinary education. The tar incident proved it. With growing respect his fellow workers made oblique inquiry about his life before he came to the stave mill. The questions were politely parried with answers that gave no information. The gossipers concluded that he came from "the coast," probably New Orleans and was "educated." Most accepted the account and asked no more questions.

Word of the natural-resin-tar spread and soon other stockmen were asking for it. The slack winter season provided spare time, so with the permission of his employer, Tar set up a permanent cooker.

Rich resin wood was plentiful at first. Later, as Tar ranged further afield, the heavy loads became too difficult to lug. A friend came by for a gallon of tar and upon seeing Tar struggling with a load, suggested that he would sell him a young female donkey and a two-wheeled cart for five dollars each. A deal was done and within a week, Kate, a small jenny was hauling Tar's resin wood.

His new more efficient operation soon produced more resin tar that the local community consumed. Tar and Kate then went "on the road" peddling their product to other locals where it found a ready market.

This natural tar was used as a salve or ointment on livestock for cuts, abrasions, bruises, infections, insecticide, and even as a paint for short term identification. Canvas was created when it was applied to cotton cloth. When mixed with sulphur, cattle could be dosed with the mixture for a variety of colds and distemper. Skiffs and watering troughs were caulked with cotton and tar to stop leaks. Mangy dogs were covered with it. Squeaky wagon axles were quieted when it was added to lard and applied to the bearings.

Also, it became an essential part of home medical remedies, and was applied to people in as many ways as to livestock. For example: A drop or two mixed with sugar would purge kids of intestinal worms. When thinned with turpentine or kerosene it stopped the itch of scabies. A dab on a boil, backed with a cotton cloth to prevent smearing, brought the boil to a "head" for lancing. If daubed over a ring worm ravaged area of the skin, the parasite vanished. A little added to sulphur, molasses, and a slug of moonshine created a good spring tonic which, of course, everyone needed. The writer remembers it as an ingredient in the potent mixture saturated into flannel cloths to be applied over kids' chests for colds. This flannel cloth, pinned inside our long handled underwear, was lethal to self-esteem. Fumes, generated by body heat, rose in an unending odoriferous vapor that alerted all with smelling range that you were sick. There were many other applications and it seemed that the only limit to the use of Tar's tar was the limit of human imagination.

We thought it was a necessary and vital part of farm life six decades ago but today if you desired some medicinal tar it would be hard to find.

Tar's age and his ailment (rumored to be skin cancer but not openly discussed in those days because of taboo) caused his peddling forays to be spaced further apart. After more than a decade of travel with Kate, Tar stopped calling.

A recent query to an elderly friend revealed that Tar is buried back in the hills in a community cemetery. The friend remembers Tar as the man who let him ride Kate to the spring for water when he was six. Also he recalled that Tar was hard working, honest, and a gentleman whose product was always of good quality and supplied at an affordable and predictable price.

Tar, a man of some mystery is still remembered by a few people. No one knows what happened to Kate.

Sam and the Dinner Bell

> *Some Homer of the cotton fields should sing the saga of the mule and of his place in the South. He it was, more than any other creature or thing, who steadfast to the land when all else faltered before thehopeless juggernaut of circumstance, impervious to conditions that broke men's hearts because of him venomous and patient preoccupation with the immediate present, won the prone South from beneath the iron heel of reconstruction and taught it pride again through humility, and courage through adversity overcome;—*
>
> William Faulkner - <u>Sartoris</u> Part 4

SAM'S LONG BROWN EARS moved to and fro as though searching for a sound. Then they wrung to his left as he aimed them. He abruptly stopped and stood like a bird dog on point. Boots, his driver and master, thought Sam had twitched his ears to rid them of an insistent horsefly or was responding to the itch of an imbedded tick. He made a mental note to examine Sam's ears when he had the time. Bess, Sam's teammate, had heard no instruction from Boots but she also stopped and noticing Sam's "point" moved her ears and listened.

Boots slapped the rope reins against Sam's back and quietly reminded him to "Gitup" as he shifted the cultivator plows nearer to the cotton row. Sam turned his head, looked at Boots and responded by spreading his legs and urinating. After Sam had piddled, Boots flapped the reins again and demanded "Git up" in a louder commanding tone. With still no response from Sam he slapped the reins even harder and Bess  pulled the cultivator against Sam's haunches. Sam's only reaction was a quivering flick of his hide where the reins had stung. Boots, from experience, realized that Sam had balked.

Sam had balked near the middle of a hundred acre cotton field at eleven o'clock on a hot July morning while going away from the mule barn, Boots' shack and the noon rest time.

- - -

It had been a long hot morning that began at daybreak when Boots had fed each mule a dozen ears of corn and a half bale of hay. Boots had then returned to his shack for a breakfast prepared by his wife. While their three children slept he wolfed three fried eggs with pork fat-back and a half dozen biscuits with a generous pouring of sorghum molasses. The breakfast was finished with three cups of sweetened black coffee.

Upon Boots' return to the barn, Sam and Bess were bridled and led to the watering trough where Boots pumped water from the well until the mules' thirst was slaked. Boots, in turn, filled his wooden keg and then led Sam and Bess to the gear (tack) room where he tied their reins to a convenient hitching ring. With a metal currying comb he removed the mud, manure, straw, burs and other rubbish from their dark brown bodies. As Boots curried he saw that his arm, in the shadowy hallway of the barn, was the same brown as Sam and Bess. "Hello mules," he muttered and finished the grooming with a brush as Sam and Bess luxuriated in the ritual by pressing their bodies against the bristles of the brush.

The grooming finished, Boots began harnessing: first came the shoulder collars with their quilted pad backing; these were placed from beneath the neck and buckled at the top. This was followed with the wooden harness placed over the collar and secured with a leather strap and buckle from beneath. The clinking trace chains, hooked to the harness' metal fasteners, were then untangled and hung on each mule's side from the back bands. A rope plow line to the individual mule was then uncoiled from the protruding top

end of the harness and attached to a ring on the outer side of the bridle's bit. Boots then backed Sam and Bess (as a team) into place astraddle the wooden cultivator's tongue. The tongue was next attached to the harness by looping the beast chains through the ring at the tongue's end. Each mule's trace chains were, in turn, hooked to the cultivator's two single trees. The rope plow line reins were slung around Boots' neck to rest loosely on his shoulders. Sam, Bess, and Boots were then ready for a day of plodding back and forth as the three cultivated cotton in the heat of July.

On the day that Sam balked, they had cultivated cotton since seven a.m. The sun was relentlessly hot. Boots' rest stops had been frequent as he fanned himself with his big straw hat and mopped the sweat from his face, head, and neck with a flour sack sweat rag. The sloshing water in the keg, slung beneath the tongue, was almost gone. Sam and Bess were also sweaty and their deep breathing had almost become a panting. There was no breeze which allowed the gnats, flies, mosquitoes, and sweat bees to buzz around them in a pesky swarm. It was eleven o'clock by Boots' $1.00 Ingersol watch when they had begun the last round. He had guessed that he could plow another round, unhitch, walk to the barn, water and feed and arrive at his shack just in time for dinner. There might even be time for a short nap.

But Sam had balked! Boots' plans were messed up and rest, dinner and a nap would be delayed.

Boots sat on the cultivator shaft and quietly rested as he mulled over Sam's obstinacy. The insects buzzed; the mules breathed; Boots' heart thumped away in the quietness. The rural 1920s countryside had none of the noise of the modern day except sometimes the shrill whistle of a steam train engine or the deep bass of a steam boat.

And then, in the quiet, Boots heard it! "Ding, dong. Ding, dong. Ding, dong," someone was ringing a dinner bell before twelve o'clock. The sound came from over toward the Munsey place.

Boots had heard that the Munsey's were going to shorten their work day to save the mules from the mid-day heat; but this had not been confirmed. Their early bell would disrupt all the plow crews within hearing. The mules would be especially affected, since ringing bells signaled food, water, rest, and shade. Sam, especially, in his stubborn mule intelligence, had developed a strong association with bells and the good things of his life. His conditioned reflexes were much more developed than even Pavlov's dogs. No way would he "un-balk" until he was unhitched for his noonday rest.

Boots understood his own predicament. He could dispute, argue, plead, whip, or beat Sam but he knew it would achieve nothing. So in resignation he rose from his rest, unhitched and pulled the harness back to the cultivator, then he untied the plow lines and crawled astride Sam's wet sweaty back. Sam instantly became cooperative and walked away from the cultivator.

As he rode the "un-balked" Sam to dinner, with Bess trailing, Boots observed, "Ain't no use a-tryin' to plow when the mule done balked. If boss man don't like us to quit early, he can come try hisself to get Sam to plow after he done heard a bell."

The Ultimate Compliment

It came my way when my grandson, Drew McWilliams, wrote a theme in the style of me, his grandfather, "Buddy Pal" McWilliams.

He is a fifth grade student with imagination and I'm proud of him.

This story is presented for your enjoyment. It is slightly edited for ease of typing.

(The Big House was the old Goodloe Plantation home that stood near Cherokee, Alabama, until dismantled because restoration was beyond a reasonable cost. Drew has seen pictures of it and also the material from it that is incorporated into our new home. It has enlivened his imagination.)

The Big House
By Drew McWilliams
03/10/92

Along in the early 1800s a man named Calvin Goodloe migrated across the Atlantic to America. He went many places looking for a good place to settle. He came along a place in Northwest Alabama near the Tennessee River in

Colbert County and bought it. He built a cabin there about 1830 married and had a son, Calvin, Jr.

5 yrs. Past - his cabin turned into a large house and kept growing - around 1850 he died, but his son kept building and bought slaves. He kept on buying until the house was a large mansion about 1855. Now he owned a pretty big plantation from the top of the mountain to the river which is about 5 miles from the mountain. He married and lived a life of luxury till the war broke out in 1861. So he went to fight with the Union. (Rumor has it that he was a congressman in D.C. and found it convenient to remain there - Buddy Pal's note). That year gun boats traveled up the Tennessee River. Florence a town about 10 miles up stream was taken. Shots could be heard for at least 5 miles in every direction. They could be heard down and up river about 15 miles away. They may have been heard in Iuka. The next city taken was Decatur, then Huntsville. Meanwhile on the plantation the man's wife tried to take care of it. Almost a year later Union soldiers came up river with troops they came on the plantation and used the mansion as a headquarters. There are still gun barrel marks on the doors when they tried to burst the doors down. One morning in 1862 the troops set out for a scout of the area and at the bottom of the mountains the confederate met them and they had a small battle with only a few shots. At my house today I found a cannon ball. We think they camped at the place. Back to the mansion: After the war the slaves were free and the Goodloe mansion remained silent for many years, nearly 60 years. In the early 1920s my great grandfather W. McWilliams bought it and liven there for many years. My Grandfather, James "Buddy Pal" McWilliams grew up there he has told me many stories about living there. I will tell you some of my favorites titles: The Pantuh Scare, Monster Cat, and The Old Brick Haul. The Pantuh Scare starts like this: One night great grandpas dogs were barking but after awhile they stopped. They did this thing for 2 nights. Then, the 3rd night my great grandfather went to see what was wrong, he heard something growl and he screamed ran in

the house got his pistol saying "it's a pantuh he ran outside pointed his pistol and "click," "click" "click" he screamed. By the time he got inside and back with the revolver loaded this time it was gone. This next story is called "Monster Cat!" In the early 1920s every farmer had a top cat. On our farm it was a big tom cat named Monster he ruled the farm. They had an old smoke house full of meat. Monster kept raiding it. One day though my great grandfather caught him in the act. The battle had begun my great grandfather got a shovel while Monster ran down the hung up meat but he couldn't get out but through the door that great grandfather guarded. Monster made way to the door running over the meat. Great Grandfather swung again and again, but missed and finally his hat fell off pausing as his bald head was uncovered. His eyes pleaded to the cat not to jump (How True), but it was a good get away. Then occurred the leap to great grandpa's head to let out a scream and the cat was gone. They never saw Monster again.

This story is my favorite its called The Old Brick Haul.

In the 1920s

My Great Grandfather was making a brick shed out of bricks from Tuscumbia. He usually got half a ton at a time, but wanted to finish today so he cranked his old dodge truck and headed for Tuscumbia. He stopped midway for gas. He knew the store owner and said he would carry 3 tons. The store owner said you better not try it. Great Grandpa cranked the dodge and when he got to Tuscumbia he loaded the truck with nearly 3½ tons and he headed back to Cherokee saying to his truck come on you can make it thinking "I hope the tires doesn't go flat." He made it to the farm and to his house and was about to back up. My grandfather was 10 years old with a fire cracker tooked his eyes off the truck onto the fire crackers lit it and threw it in a can closed his eyes and plugged his ears. But later he thought "That's an old gas can!" "Boom!" the firecracker went. My Great Grandfather cut the truck off got out kicked the tire and screamed. My grandfather asked "what's wrong." Great Grandfather replied, "The truck has a flat." My grandfather said that was a firecracker. <u>Great Grandfather started a chase.</u>

It remained silent. Then my grandfather bought it in the early 1960s tore it down and built a house over it. The huge basement is still there. The sistern (cistern) is now a swimming pool and while they were tearing down a staircase my grandfather tore a hole in one and money came falling down - 1800s money. (Pal's note - actually we found fifty half dollars and two quarters - all predating the Civil War.)

Frosting on the Cake:

My Grand daughter Katie also caught the writing bug.
She is eight and in the third grade. Her poems are dear to my heart.

Enjoy:

Everybody Says
    Everybody says I look like my mother
    and I'm taller than my brother
    But I don't see
    Why I can't look like me?
To Linda - By Katie

    I Heard a Bird sing
    I heard a bird sing December
    December
    Now remember!
    It's not September or November
    So remember - It's December
To Sesa - By Katie

First Snow

When the snow falls
The bushes feel like popcorn balls
The places I play
Don't seem like yesterday
And the winds blow,
and release snow.

                                        To Cathy - By Katie

The Christmas of 1929

"For Christmas comes but once a year".
             Thomas Tusser, 1524-1580
             Chapter 12 - The Farmer's Daily Diet

THAT YEAR, when I was nine, I spent all my free-time with the three Hardie brothers; Lee, John, and Luke. Their ages were eight, nine, and ten. The brothers and I had the best year of our young lives - perhaps of our entire lives - that year.

Hours were spent at the old swimming hole dog-paddling about or splashing into the clear water from the rope swing we had hung from a convenient tree limb. Our skin often became water-wrinkled from over-exposure to the wetness.

As make-believe pirates, each had a treasure box filled with fancy rocks, Indian arrow points, marbles, old costume jewelry, chalk, and other "valuable" junk. These treasures were cleverly hidden about the farm Afterwards, individual pirates would carefully disclose clues until all the treasures were found. "Treasure hunt" was a game no one tired of playing.

If chores interfered, all four pitched in so as to rescue our playmate from his enslavement. Play was of utmost importance to us.

We knew where the old Indian villages had been and collected arrow points, larger spear points, bluestone tomahawks, broken pottery, and even old bone needles. Boxes of these artifacts, sitting in closets, still remind me of those bygone days.

In our roaming about, we climbed cliffs and explored caves. Nuts cascaded from walnut and hickory trees when we climbed into the branches and shook them, Nothing tastes better than black walnuts or hickory nuts before a fire, on a cold winter's night. We ate persimmons and wild 'possum grapes, straight from the tree and vine. We gigged frogs with small barbed spears made from straightened fish hooks. This sport sometimes degenerated into snake snaring so that we could shock parents - or girls - with snakes coiled in clear glass fruit jars. We fished. We made toys at the farm shop. We built small log cabins. We dammed the creek to install miniature water paddle wheels. We fought make-believe cowboy and Indian wars.

We four lucky farm boys led an idealistic life that year.

But we wanted things: We wanted Keds tennis shoes like those worn by our town cousins so as to avoid the thorns and cuts to our bare feet. We wanted bicycles for faster access to the swimming hole and other play places. We wanted candy, store-bought cake, licorice sticks, ice cream, soda pop, and other junk food. We wanted the new fancy overalls with the high side buttons. We wanted - we wanted - we wanted.

Most of all, I wanted an air rifle: each Hardie brother had a Daisy air rifle that held five-hundred BBs in its magazine. One loading would last for a full day of imaginary big game-hunting or plinking. The Hardies' let me tag along with my ordinary rubber-band powered sling-shot as they shot lizards, toads, snakes, bugs, tin cans, and, sometimes, birds. On one foray, they let me shoot a rat that had been plowed from its den in an open field. After three attempts, I hit it and knew my calling! I was a natural rifleman and should be a scout for the U.S. Cavalry just like Tom Mix of movie fame.

Waves of yearning, desire, and longing for an air-rifle possessed me. Thus driven, I began a campaign to own a rifle by Christmas morning. Dad was informed of my great need. Grandpa was given notice. A favorite unmarried uncle was included. And finally, but most importantly, I pled my cause to Mamaw, my stepmother.

Later, on a visit to kinfolk in town, I saw a <u>Boy's Life</u> magazine that had an advertisement for a thousand shot King air-rifle. "Genuine black-walnut-looking stock, with five thousand BBs included, for just six dollars", the advertisement proclaimed. A picture of the rifle spread over the back page with a happy smiling boy admiring it. "Price good until November fifteenth", urged the advertisement.

With permission, I removed the page, fetched it home, and hung it on the door to the family boy's room. It was a constant reminder that brought about good results.

My uncle, Alvie, gave my a dollar on his pay-day. By the first week in November, I had added four more dollars in pennies, nickels, and dimes. Then Dad, after a conversation with Mamaw, suggested that I fill out the order because he would give me the rest of the money.

I met the mailman that Saturday morning with the completed order and enough cash to buy the necessary mail money order, an envelope, and a three-cent stamp. Mr. Chambers, the mailman addressed the envelope for me, placed the papers inside, moistened the flap and sealed it. He licked the stamp, stuck it on the envelope, and tossed my dream order into a box on the seat of his Ford. Everything was done except the waiting.

No one told me when the rifle arrived by parcel post on a school day. Regular Saturday meetings with Mr. Chambers resulted in evasive answers. Later, I learned that Dad had instructed him to keep the delivery a secret; this was to forestall my nagging about the rifle. My other brothers and sisters were getting no gifts before Christmas - neither should I. Later, Dad reassured me by explaining: "You'll get the rifle on Christmas morning."

There was that long waiting: until, on Christmas morning all we farm people arose an hour earlier than usual so as to finish the chores before daylight and gift opening time. When we trudged outside, a soft, generous snowfall was drifting down with flakes like millions of tiny white feathers. The flakes settled on grass stems, tree twigs, and stuck persistently to our clothing. It was all a silent whiteness - a perfect white Christmas.

By six o'clock the crew had milked the cows - cleaned the barn - loaded the milk delivery truck - let the calves suckle the nurse cows - brought in firewood - fed the mules - fed the hogs - mixed cottonseed meal and ground ear corn for the afternoon's milking - shoveled the snow from doorways - washed the milk buckets - and were ready for breakfast and Christmas.

When the chores were finished, I asked, "Dad, can I have my rifle now?"

"You sure can," he answered and reached for a long red ribboned cardboard box behind our cedar Christmas tree. My family watched as I tore open one end and slid the black-walnut-looking stock into view, followed by the loading lever mechanism and then the long lustrous black, metallic barrel. A search inside the box found five, one-thousand-shot packets of BBs.

Six decades and more have not diminished the clarity of my remembrance.

The soft fall of ghostly snow continued as the darkness held the dawn at bay, I couldn't wait. My oatmeal was gulped down as I stuffed two sausage biscuits into the bib pockets of my overalls. A woolen 'boggan cap was pulled over my head and ears as I jammed my arms into the sleeves of my winter coat. With rifle in my arms and BBs in my pockets, I ran out into the snowy dawning of a perfect Christmas.

The only sound was the crunching of my shoes in the snow as I made my way to the Hardie's dog-trot style log home. Large flakes stuck to my 'boggan and tickled my nose and cheeks. Woodsmoke mingled with the breakfast smell of bacon, eggs, coffee, and oatmeal as the fragrance was wafted on the still air. When I approached the Hardie's home, Ol' Snuff, their hound, recognized my scent - or walk - and didn't bark. The one-thousand shot King rifle with its long barrel balanced perfectly in my sock mittened grasp. The three Hardies would be overwhelmed by its elegant design and large capacity magazine. The euphoria of a perfect day's beginning gave me a sense of magic that was beyond understanding - and still is.

The Hardies waited before the open hearth fire as they turned themselves to avoid scorched overalls. Their Daisies were oiled and loaded, ready for adventure. But first, they admired my thousand-shot King rifle with the black-walnut-looking stock and its long barrel. However, the admiration was brief because we had adventure waiting for us in the white snowy dawn.

When we went outside, the snow laden clouds and falling flakes filtered and diffused the meager light into a shadowless glow. The dawning resembled a mid-summer's gloaming magic. It was enchantment to four little boys who seldom saw snow.

Animal tracks were visible, especially rabbits; we followed the tracks to hiding places and exuberantly shot at bunnies as they disappeared into the snowy whiteness.

Floating leaves down at the swimming hole resembled pirate ships and were sunk by our cannons on shore. Nuts remaining on trees became enemy formations of aircraft that fluttered down in imaginary flames when BBs exploded into make-believe shrapnel near them. Enemy submarines were sunk as tin cans cruised down the creek and were shattered by batteries of Daisy and King cannons.

Time and reality was forgotten as my trusty one-thousand shot King rifle with its walnut look-alike stock and long, black, lustrous, metallic barrel, sporting a front-beaded and rear-notched blade sight, also including a frontier Winchester-type lever action and I roamed the unexplored far North frontiers with its arctic-like wilderness. My three scouts with their lesser Daisy rifles carefully remained within the protective range of my King rifle as we warriors slowly advanced into the perilous unknown of the frozen snow covered arctic tundra — habitat of the aliens.

I wish Christmas still came once each year.

Rocks in Our Yard
or
Stone Unhinged

Stonehenge - Ston henj - A notable example of the ancient stone sicles, near Wiltshire, England — probably — suggest to some — that it was connected with the worship of the sun.
                                        Encyclopedia Americana

WHEN SOME PEOPLE SEE THEM the first time, they ask, "Why did you carve them into such queer shapes?" Sometimes they are less polite and ask, "Who's the strange, deranged sculptor?" Most simply inquire, "Where'd you get them crazy rocks?"

Our grandchildren on the farm and their visitors play among them at every opportunity. Even the cattle often congregate next to them at sundown for the comfort and seeming security of their company. And, after years of their presence, I still occasionally walk among them.

The rocks, with "crazy" shapes, of course, were carved by mother nature and are here after a creative process going back billions of years.

However, they were erected in our front yard because of

the dinosaur fad occurring over the past few decades. Children were given toys, books, movies, and visits to museums that featured the dinosaur and it's history. One grandchild became an expert and could rattle off dinosaur names such as "Bronosaurus-mousequtious regal" or "Habilitusmotionus sibilus minor" as easily as they reeled off the name of "Ol' Ranger", the yard dog.

The first rock we set in concrete was identified by my six-year-old grandson, Drew. He said it resembled a herbivorous dinosaur because its neck was long and arched for flexibility, making it easy to reach foliage when grazing. He gave it the name herbivorous something-or-other. Later, and nearby, we found a smaller version with similar body configuration - even to the neck - and set it near the larger rock. Our herbivorous something-or-other became a female with a calf.

I take credit for the large Neanderthal man with massive head and shoulders. It had been in my path for years until one day I discovered its identity all at once (somebody said, "...and the eye begins to see"). Anyway, we assured his permanent uprightness with a heavy steel rod set in reinforced concrete. His body of stone personifies physical strength and stands over the group.

Katie, a granddaughter, was four when we found the large rabbit. She exuberantly helped to pry him from the ground with a steel bar heavier than her weight. The rabbit now sits in rabbit-like awareness ready to bound away at the slightest provocation even though he is anchored in concrete and weighs a quarter-of-a-ton.

Wendy was twelve and helped discover the road-runner and place him before the other stone figures. There was no debate when we stood him vertically for identification; he was obviously a road-runner. His sassy impertinent beak and head, with the hint of a plume, were balanced with a rudder-like tail. All was built for speed. The resemblance to the road-runner of cartoon and T.V. fame is eerie as he stands there in full arrested speed.

Ol' John, our grandson, helped set up each stone when

his busy schedule permitted. Growing into teenage strength, he was often needed. The friar, with the large pointed hood over his head and neck, stands in quiet strength reigning over the boisterous group of rocks. John and the friar share the trait of quiet confidence.

A sea-going mammal resembles an otter, or perhaps an elephant seal, or maybe a pre-whale. It seems to slither with undulations in mud and water. Its unusual length required concrete at the front flippers and a steel anchor rod at the rear. In imagination we can almost see and hear the sight and sound of an ancient swampy lake.

An aboriginal mother totes her baby in a shoulder pack as she trudges behind the Neanderthal - or is it a porpoise leaping from the sea with a large open mouth?

Waddling beside the rabbit is a stone duck with a long bill and a short stubby rump. He struggles to keep up as he sits there in concrete.

A stone bird sits on a post with long, rusty legs of iron rod and leans into the breeze ready for flight.

A bull-dog-like canine stone figure is out front blazing the trail for the group. He may be a replica of the wer-wolf of ancient lore, believed to have existed before man and dog became friends.

It's a mystery as to why so many unusual limestone figures were created on our acre of exposed rock. Maybe a meteorite shattered it and started the erosion, the leaching, and the smoothing. Who knows?

Scientists remind us that a vast inconceivable time was expended in the creation: continents drifted thousands of miles - oceans rose and fell hundreds of feet - meteors and asteroids crashed - life began, then waxed and waned - glaciers accumulated as large as continents, melted and then accumulated again, over and over - land masses buckled into mountains that were then eroded away - volcanoes spewed dust, lava, and gases over the surface and into the atmosphere - torrential rains fell for centuries - heat - cold - radiation - magnetic reversal - tides - sun spots - chemical processes and, probably, many unknown forces were involved. All acted and reacted - again and again - to create our limestone rocks that are mostly made from the skeletal remains of billions upon trillions of life forms. Our rock menagerie marches from an unknown past into an unknown future. It stirs the imagination.

For example: imagine: it is October of the year 3992, short two-thousand-years from now. A group of five-hundred-year-old senior citizens wheel themselves into a semi-circle 'round our rock menagerie, still standing, protected by a large, clear, plastic dome filled with an inert gas to prevent oxidation and weather erosion. Each senior site encased in a mobile, life-sustaining medical-module. The leader thumps his microphone and admonishes the group, "Take a few deep breaths of pure oxygen so that your brain receptors will be refreshed." He then explains that they, as senior citizens of the Great Society in the Fortieth Century, need to know how their primitive ancestors of the Twentieth Century had lived. He continues, "Part of this understanding can come from viewing the stone figures before you, which are composed of the skeletal remains of uncounted life forms. Their unintended deaths created these figures and the primitives - knowing this - practiced a form of idol worship before them, thankful that *their* skeletons were not yet fossils. Our ancestors, it is thought, carried on rites among the stone. If you will observe, one figure up front has a natural cleavage or hole through the stone. Also, note that the figures all face to the southwest at an exact angle of twenty-three degrees, twenty-seven minutes from due west. As the sun went down on the day of the winter solstice, it is thought, our primitives placed themselves so that the sun's rays, shining though the cleavage, would strike their smiling faces. This act, supposedly assured them happiness for a full year. Any questions?", the leader concludes.

Primitive reader, please, just one small smile and you may let the sun's rays shine on your face through the hole in the stone at the next winter's solstice.

The Reunion

"The soldier above all other people prays for peace, for he must suffer and bear the deepest wounds and scars of war."
Douglas McArthur

THEY GATHERED again, after a half-century has flown by, in an attempt to remember the time when they as young men, were violently taught that they too were not immortal - a time when death was a daily companion.

Name badges identified those old airmen as former companions; but, time had blurred and wrinkled their faces until only a close scrutiny could recognize them. Often a name was remembered but the gray-haired, stooped, old man was not. Name badges were consulted again and again as they leafed through the picture albums of World War II.

They gathered from all parts of America - from Fort Worth, Long Island, Ponotoc, Pine Top, Cherokee, Portland, San Diego, Miami, and all points between. Many had continued life as airmen in the armed services or as civilians. A few were veterans of Korea, Vietnam, and the smaller wars. They had continued an active life and were exceptionally well informed. Time had added wisdom to their many other attributes.

Their first "gathering" had been in the early 1940s at Air Force bases in Louisville, Kentucky; Sedalia, Kansas; Fayetteville, North Carolina; Fort Wayne, Indiana; Nottingham, England; and, finally, Welford park, England, where they became operational. After becoming fully staffed, personnel changed constantly through the normal attrition of military operation. There is an old military adage, "Here today and gone tomorrow". However, the majority remained together long enough to become fast friends.

And now, a half-century later, they were gathering again at the Sheraton in New Orleans. A few key airmen had planned, in detail, a perfect reunion. Old airmen became reacquainted in an ideal setting.

"Do you remember?" was a constant query: that skinny, old, arthritic, seventy-five-year-old man sitting quietly there remembered! He had flown the English Channel in a C47 loaded with ammunition for Patton and landed at a makeshift airstrip, under fire, again and again - even after his plane had bullet holes and after he was numb with fatigue.

"Do you remember?" - That short, fat, eighty-year-old man, animatedly talking on our right, had been a radio operator who watched as a platoon of paratroopers jumped behind the German lines. His plane then took a direct hit and he had followed the troopers down. He became a prisoner of war.

"Do you remember?" - A survivor of the crash that took the lives of all his crew sits silently listening, as he remembers. After the Battle of the Bulge, he had returned to the squadron for reassignment lugging a P-38 pistol taken from a German officer.

"Do you remember?" - A haze had hidden the airport at Marrakesh, Morocco, and one plane, short of fuel, had landed in the desert. The next day, they were able to take off and later found the airport with only ten minutes of fuel remaining. They remember.

"Do you remember?" - The fish and chips at the train station in Reading, England, were especially good eating after the train ride from London at midnight.

"Do you remember?" - Those three army trucks, that wrecked in the fog outside Reading, killed three men and hospitalized several more. Those who were there remember.

"Do you remember?" - One night a British Sterling bomber attempted to land on the base at Welford and crashed killing all the crew. The explosion blew out a few windows in the barracks and unhooked the blackout curtains.

"Do you remember?" - A squadron of B26 circled low over Welford and began landing at less than minute intervals. Fog had closed their home base and any landing was better then a crash. Their tires screeched and skidded as they applied brakes on the short runway and then taxied onto the open field to avoid a pile up. After our C47s returned, all parking and taxi strips were loaded with planes.

"Do you remember?" - The ground crews were flown to France late one afternoon and off-loaded at an abandoned Luftwaffe base near Paris. They were instructed to remain where they were until the next morning because of the danger of German booby traps. It was as cold as a brass monkey so they damn near did.

"Do you remember?" - There were so many bombers flying just before the invasion that their vapor trails created a complete overcast on an otherwise clear day. The thousands of motors reverberated until the earth seemed to quiver under our feet.

"Do you remember?" - A glider disintegrated after a plane had towed it to an altitude of two thousand feet. The crew and all equipment, including a Jeep, plummeted into the ground.

"Do you remember?" - A crew and plane were lost in North Carolina. One crew member, Sgt. Knowlton, occupied the bunk next to the writer, who gathered the Sergeant's belongings and also wrote a letter to his fiance.

"Do you remember?" - Those anti-sub guns that were manned as the ship zig-zagged across the North Atlantic were manned by amateurs. An officer instructed, "Point them at anything that looks like a periscope and pull the trigger. The gun will do the rest". At night the phosphorescent water and the flying fish skipping through the wave crests was sight this writer will never forget.

"Do you remember?" - - "Do you remember?" - - - "Do you remember?" - - - -

The youngest man at the reunion was sixty-eight going on sixty-nine. The oldest was eighty-five going on eighty-four. They plan to meet next year in Colorado — probably at Colorado Springs near the Air Force Academy. There will be a poignant memorial ceremony for those who no longer ask, "Do you remember?"

In Memory Of Our Fellow Airmen Who Made The Supreme Sacrifice, We Hold Our First Reunion

78th SQUADRON

MAJOR CHARLES K. BOYD	CAPT. PAUL C. JOYSLIN
CAPT. THOMAS TOMENY	1ST. LT. HALE L. WATSON
2ND. LT. HARROL H. JACKS	2ND. LT. MARTIN H. KEHOE
2ND. LT. HOWARD R. JOHNSON, JR.	2ND. LT. RICHARD G. SHIPLEY
2ND. LT. JOHN F. REYNOLDS	2ND. LT. ROBERT G. WHITE
2ND. LT. CHARLES A. SMITH, JR.	2ND. LT. WALTER L. GREEN
2nd. LT. RICHARD J. WRIGHT	FLT./O. SYLVESTER H. KEMPEN
FLT./O. WILLIAM P. O'HAVER	FLT./O. NORMAN T. LUND
FLT./O. WILLIAM T. McCABE	FLT./O. ROBERT P. DAVIS
FLT./O. WILLIAM A. HEELAS	FLT./O. LEONARD O. HYMAN
SGT. ROBERT M. ANDERSON	S/SGT. RAYMOND G. SIEVERT
SGT. LEONARD J. GOUGEON	SGT. ROGER H. KNOWLTON
SGT. ROBERT B. CRAVEN	SGT. JAMES O'KANE
CPL. ROY A. ROBY	CPL. MELVIN C. PERIALAS

May We Never Forget What These Men Sacrificed For Mankind.

About the Author - By the Author

I AM A SEVENTY-TWO-YEAR-OLD RETIRED FARMER from the northwest corner of Alabama where I have lived all my life. The oldest in a farm family with two brothers and five sisters, Sarah and I have three children of our own and seven grandchildren. There are uncounted kinfolk living near and far.

Except for a brief stint in the army and an even shorter college exposure, I have always lived on a farm. Farm life has made me, of necessity, a jack-of-all-trades. I am an amateur mechanic, electrician, welder, carpenter, surveyor, architect, chemist, geneticist, lawyer, etc. Even on occasion there were "letters to the editor" written by an amateur.

Reading is an obsession with me; I read the cereal box at breakfast. Odds and ends collect in my mind and make me a "pack-rat" for scraps and fragments of second-hand experience.

My philosophical persuasions tend toward classic liberalism. My mentors are such people as: B. Franklin, T. Jefferson, Voltaire, T. Paine, A. Rand, and M. Thatcher. Individual freedom is more important then the so-called freedom of special groups. It follows that capitalism is the only workable economic system.

Three years in the Army Air Force taught me the universality of human aspirations and, also, made me aware of the slender, tenuous thread that supports all life on this small planet in the vastness of space. We are all "terminal".

And yet, I agree with the optimist and do not accept the demise of the human race. The struggle toward consciousness, knowledge, and reality will continue and we will move to a higher understanding.

I have hope.

And hope is the difference. I am an optimist at age seventy-two, even though I understand the Bureau of Vital Statistics tables of survivability.

Live!

Signed

Jimmie McWilliams

ORDER FORM

To order additional copies of *Cornpone,* please fill out this order form and send it to:

D.R. Virtue Press
3215 Asphalt Rock Road
Route 1, Box 301 A
Cherokee, Alabama 35616

Please enclose a check or money order for $19.95 per book, plus $2.05 shipping and handling per book.

- -

ORDER FORM

Name: _____

Address: _____

City: _____

State: _____ Zip: _____

Phone: (_____) _____

Quantity of books: _____ at $19.95 each = _____

Shipping and handling at $2.05/each = _____

Alabama residents add 4% sales tax: _____

TOTAL: _____

D.R. Virtue Press

3215 Asphalt Rock Road
Route 1, Box 301 A
Cherokee, Alabama 35616